1787

1·7·8·7

A NOVEL BY

JOAN ANDERSON

WITH ILLUSTRATIONS BY

ALEXANDER FARQUHARSON

Harcourt Brace & Company

Orlando Atlanta Austin Boston San Francisco Chicago Dallas New York
Toronto London

This edition is published by special arrangement with Harcourt Brace & Company.

For permission to reprint copyrighted material, grateful acknowledgment is made to the following sources:

Harcourt Brace & Company: *1787* by Joan Anderson, illustrated by Alexander Farquharson. Text copyright © 1987 by Joan Anderson; illustrations copyright © 1987 by Harcourt Brace & Company.

The Newborn Group: Cover illustration by Teresa Fasolino from *1787* by Joan Anderson.

Printed in the United States of America

ISBN 0-15-308398-0

4 5 6 7 8 9 10   026   03 02 01

TO R. D. W.

—J.A.

ACKNOWLEDGMENTS

I wish to thank the following:

My agent, Susan Cohen, who introduced me to the possibility of writing historical fiction; Willa Perlman, who conceived the project and had faith that I could carry it forth; Erin Gathrid, my editor, who helped bring the manuscript to life; David Kimball, Constitutional Historian, whose knowledge of the document, its times, and the men who wrote it enabled me to bring truth and accuracy to this book; Martha Masterson, to whom I came to refer as my literary shrink because she listened and encouraged me every step of the way; Dan Masterson, a good friend and fellow writer, who read the original proposal and gave me a push; the entire Pearl River Library staff, especially Carolyn Johnson for her advice on dialect, Jerry Rosinski for her reference help, and Anita Joeckle for always being there.

I am most grateful to Dr. C. Kenneth Snyder, a political science whiz, for his valuable character references and for pointing the way to common sense; Audrey and Steve Simpson of Philadelphia, who guided me to all the important places and introduced me to all the right people; and Kate Learson of New York City, who allowed me to hide in her apartment long enough to get the manuscript on its way.

Special appreciation goes to the fifty-five founding fathers, who worked so hard during those one hundred days to produce one of the world's most significant documents.

Joan Anderson, December, 1986

PROLOGUE

"GIDDAP," the driver shouted as his whip cut across the horse's back. "Giddap!"

The coach pulled away from the curved gravel driveway in front of the Mifflin mansion with a jolt. Jared waved good-bye. Uncle Thomas had just given him one of his customary pats on the back; it was the kind of man-to-man pat that left Jared rubbing his neck afterward.

He could see Aunt Sarah dab at her eyes, trying not to let Jared see her sadness as the coach rumbled up the cobblestone street. He turned his body around to peer through the sliver of a back window, his eyes locked on his adoptive family until they were out of sight.

As a mixture of emotions flooded over him, Jared positioned himself so that he had a good view of Market Street. If all went according to plan, Hetty Morris would be casually standing on her front stoop. Jared would not be home from Princeton until well after winter; and on this particular early September morning, that seemed like forever.

His stomach tightened as the coach rounded the corner of Sixth Street. Hetty had promised to wear her frilly blue dress. If for some reason she was detained inside, they had arranged that she would wave her handkerchief from the drawing room window.

Jared had not yet even glanced at the others sharing the crowded coach. His entire being was focused on the next few moments. In fact, all morning, while Margaret served his favorite breakfast and Annie tucked last-minute necessities into his trunk and Uncle Thomas gave him another set of final instructions, he had not really noticed or heard a thing. Seeing Hetty one more time was all that mattered.

The coach moved slowly up the slight incline that signaled the approach to the Morris home. Jared's heart skipped a beat as he strained for a glimpse of blue. He found himself wishing that the Morris house were on the incline rather than at the top of it—that way, when they passed by the moment would last longer.

Then he saw her—so regal and lovely. At five feet tall, Hetty was tiny, delicately featured. As always her chestnut-colored hair was pulled back from her softly freckled face, and long curls peeked from under her bonnet. Suddenly she began waving her arms frantically, motioning to the coachman to stop. Jared could not imagine what she was up to.

"Halt," the driver called out as the carriage ground to a stop. "I'm sorry, ma'am," Jared heard the driver say. "We are all full up. Next coach for up north won't be 'round till the morning."

"Oh, I needn't a seat, sir," Hetty said in her most dainty voice. "I have a message for one of your passengers . . . a Jared Mifflin, sir. So sorry to be troubling you, sir, but I'd be most obliged if you could give this to him."

Jared felt sure that had this been anyone but pretty little Hetty, the driver would not have lingered a minute longer. "He's in the back, missy, so you can hand it to him yourself," he said. "Hurry up now, or I'll be off my schedule."

Jared leaned out the window. His eyes never left Hetty's as she slipped the envelope into his hand. They said nothing to each other. With that brief touch, she withdrew her hand, and the coach pulled abruptly away.

Jared strained his body peering out the back window until Hetty was no longer there. Folding the perfumed note, he placed it in his breast pocket. When he finally looked around at the other passengers, the two portly gentlemen sitting across from him were smiling, and one of them even winked. Jared blushed. Very few people knew the depth of his feelings for Hetty. They had been so clever most of the summer—trying not to draw attention to their relationship—until the Fourth of July celebration at the Bartram estate. Only Henry and William really knew what had gone on.

A smile spread across Jared's face as he leaned his head back and thought of the many things that only the four of them knew. They had been witnesses to history, and it had all begun on that muggy Sunday in May.

CHAPTER ONE

IT was May thirteenth, Sunday to be precise. Weekly church attendance was expected of all respectable Philadelphian families. But on that day, there was an incentive for putting up with the hot, stuffy three-hour service that lay ahead. After church, Jared had arranged to meet Hetty Morris privately—for the first time. Even though their families had known each other for as long as Jared could remember, it had taken him months to even speak to Hetty, and then another month before he found the nerve to ask her to spend Sunday afternoon with him.

As Jared dressed that morning, he had a hard time choosing which jacket to wear. His dark blue velveteen was the most dashing. Aunt Sarah had it specially made for him in New York. But with such stifling weather, would he not be wise to forgo elegance for comfort? As he looked at his alternatives, elegance won out. Good impressions took priority today. Pleased with his decision, Jared pulled on the blue jacket.

It was snug, and he felt the material stretching to accommodate his broadening shoulders. He hadn't realized how much he'd grown since the winter months. Flexing his muscles, he gazed at his broad chest in the little mirror that sat on his dresser. *Oh, well*, he thought, *the overall appearance is passable*. And with that he straightened his lace collar and raced down the circular staircase to the drawing room, where the entire family was waiting.

"About time!" Uncle Thomas snapped; punctuality was but one of his many idiosyncrasies. Jared thought it best to answer him with an apologetic smile. As she gazed at his attire, Aunt Sarah was obviously curious. Mercifully she kept her thoughts to herself as the family climbed into the carriage for the short ride to the Meeting House.

In order to make room for Aunt Sarah sitting opposite him, Jared had to pull his knees into his already cramped body. Crowded into the corner of the carriage, he was grateful for the less than five-minute ride.

Much to Jared's chagrin, the Mifflins entered the Free Quaker Meeting House with ample time to spare. As they headed for the family pew, he heard the bell in the Christ Church tower strike ten o'clock. That was the church that Hetty and her family attended.

Three more hours, Jared thought, wondering if the Morrises were as punctual as Uncle Thomas. He wished that the two families were members of the same church. It was ridiculous that Uncle Thomas should have fallen out of favor with the *regular* Quakers just because he went off to war and became a general in Washington's army. They did continue to attend Christ Church for a while because most of the wealthy merchants worshipped there. But after the war there were enough *fighting* Quakers that they formed their own sect. *How funny,* Jared thought, *that I never cared until now where we went to church—church was church.* But with the possibility of Hetty in his life, he looked forward to any excuse to be in the same room with her—wherever that might be.

Well, there's little I can do about the state of religion in Philadelphia, he sighed, loosening his lace collar and settling his six foot frame into the hard, cramped bench. Finding it difficult to sit still, Jared edged closer to his cousin Mary, so as to benefit from the cool breeze of her fan.

The service hasn't even begun, he agonized, *and it feels like an hour has gone by.* He occupied himself by watching the other families parade in, and chuckled out loud when Jonathan Wilson passed their pew and rolled his eyes to the ceiling, indicating a similar displeasure at having to endure yet another meeting.

Amy Bartram caught his eye as she settled directly across the room with her family and several of her girlfriends. Jared enjoyed her momentary flirtation. *Amy is attractive,* he thought, *as are her friends, but none is any match for Hetty.*

With the Meeting House now filled to capacity, Speaker Graff began by reading several passages from the Bible. Jared had too much on his mind to concentrate on the scriptures: how would he escape from the family, and where would he take Hetty? Because of protocol, his choices were limited to the State House Yard and Front Street.

Jared became more anxious and nervous with each passing moment. Unexpectedly, an usher reached across him and handed a note to Uncle Thomas. After glancing at its contents, Uncle leaned over.

"Jared," he whispered, "General Washington is nearing Chester. I must leave with Mr. Varnum to meet him. I'm counting on you, my boy, to take my place at the State House. Lend a hand wherever you can," he said, patting Jared's knee as he squeezed out of the pew and proceeded down the side aisle.

This is unbelievable, Jared thought, his shoulders drooping. *I knew the general was due in Philadelphia any day, but why today, of all days!*

Just then Mr. Clymer took to his feet, feeling the need to discuss the disastrous effects of slavery. No sooner had he completed his thirty-minute discourse than Mrs. John Thatcher rose—"Feeling moved by the spirit," she said, "to share with the members several readings on the evils of drink." Normally, Jared would have been interested in the topic. However, it had been brought up at every meeting for the last four weeks. Instead he tried to calculate exactly how much time he and Hetty would be able to manage. *Let's see, a horseback ride to Chester and back, plus a round trip on Gray's Ferry, should take Uncle at least two or three hours,* he figured. *That might give us an hour together, that is, if Samuel Hastings doesn't launch into one of his weekly orations.* No sooner had the thought crossed his mind when Hastings jumped to his feet, "feeling equally moved," as he said, to say a few words. *Oh, no,* Jared moaned almost audibly, *why did I even think it? We'll be here another hour!*

He caught himself. It was bad enough not to be paying attention to what was taking place in the house of God, but then to have nasty thoughts about a person . . . poor Mr. Hastings. Jared tried to picture what it must be like working at the soap factory—stirring huge vats of lye and beef tallow, day after day, amidst the steam and stench. He lifted his head and decided to listen to Mr. Hastings, but it was too late. His thoughts expressed, Mr. Hastings was back in his seat, his head bowed in prayer like everyone else's. Jared quickly did the same.

"And now, may the grace of God be with you as you leave this place today," Speaker Graff said, and Jared hoped the good Lord wouldn't hold his straying thoughts against him. "Amen." Jared had one foot already outside the pew, ready for a quick exit, when Speaker Graff stepped to the center of the altar with one last announcement:

"I have just been informed that the Honorable George Washington is approaching the city limits. All faithful patriots are urged to take to the streets and welcome him as is befitting a man of his stature. He comes, once again, out of duty—to aid in the execution of the national Constitution for our new nation. Let us all pray for the success of this mighty task . . . Amen."

And with that, the meeting was over.

"Amen," Jared said, raising his eyes to the ceiling in gratitude. "Aunt Sarah," he whispered, "will you and the girls be able to see yourselves home? Uncle expects me to accomplish some business at the State House in his absence."

"How considerate of you, dear. Always the gentleman," Aunt Sarah replied, sounding as though Jared could do no wrong. He felt a bit guilty at her reaction, given his thoughts during the service.

"You run along and do whatever needs to be done," she said, stretching to plant a kiss on his cheek.

"Phew!" Jared wiped the perspiration from his brow, which was damp not so much from the heat, but rather from anticipation. Adjusting his coat, he made his way through the crowd, out the back door, and quickly through the wrought-iron gate that led into the Meeting House's graveyard, where he could wait for Hetty.

The Christ Church bell struck one o'clock. Hetty should have already arrived. Their service never lasted later than half after twelve. *No doubt she is stuck with a group of her mother's friends,* Jared surmised. The ladies always spent time after church catching up with one another. He never could understand how they found so much to talk about.

Pacing up and down the rows of graves, Jared seemed drawn to the names on the tombstones . . . Ewing, Thompson, Hutchins, Rittenhouse. *That's a familiar name,* he thought. Suddenly he wondered why he ever suggested this as a meeting place for a first date!

The wait was agonizing. He headed toward the big oak tree at the farthest edge of the grounds, so that no one would see him. If his friends Jonathan and Ebin spotted him hanging around the cemetery, they would think he'd lost his mind. Once on the edge of the grounds he felt less exposed, but that didn't settle his restlessness. He had begun to pace again, when his eyes became riveted to one tombstone in particular.

HERE LIES ROBERT MAKIN
BELOVED HUSBAND AND FATHER
BORN ON THE 11TH DAY OF MAY,
SEVENTEEN HUNDRED AND FIFTY-TWO
DEPARTED THIS LIFE DURING THE
WAR FOR FREEDOM
ON THE THIRD DAY OF DECEMBER,
SEVENTEEN HUNDRED AND SEVENTY-FIVE.

Jared had ceased all movement, but his eyes raced from stone to stone. They were all soldiers, all dead as a result of the Revolutionary War. Jared's lightheartedness turned to melancholy, and sad memories clouded over him.

"Jared. Jared, is that you hiding way back in that corner?" Hetty called out coyly.

"Hetty!" He swung around as though she had shaken him from a bad dream. "I thought you weren't coming," he blurted as he began to move in her direction.

"Oh dear, so sorry to worry you," she said sweetly, her voice making him relax and forget. "It wasn't easy getting away from Mother, but the most convenient thing occurred."

"Oh, yes, what?" Jared asked, glad the conversation was going so easily. He had worried about what they would say to each other.

"Well, Eliza House approached me in an agitated state. It seems she hadn't heard that General Washington was to stay at our house and not at her mother's boarding house as planned. I knew Mother would have a difficult time explaining the sudden change to Eliza, so I said, 'Mother, Eliza here says the general is staying at her mother's.' Mother was embarrassed and ruffled. I could see a lengthy conversation, or a duel, if you like, developing," Hetty giggled mischievously. "It was then that I backed away from our pew and tiptoed out the door."

"Well, it is certainly good to see you," Jared said, trying hard not to stare.

"Where should we go?" she asked without meeting his eyes. "I mean, we shouldn't stand here all day."

"I'm afraid we don't have all day, Hetty," Jared confessed. "I spent the entire time in church trying to figure out what we could do in one hour. Uncle Thomas left early to greet General Washington, and I must help out at the State House in his absence."

"Oh . . . well, I can adjust if you can. But are we to stay here in the cemetery?" She looked around, and they both giggled.

"There is a bench on the edge of the yard. It doesn't look too much different over there than the State House Yard," Jared said optimistically.

"That's perfectly fine with me," Hetty agreed. There was an awkward silence as they walked away from the dreariness. With a flutter of her fan, Hetty looked at Jared in a way which told him she thought that just being together, even in a cemetery, was wonderful.

As they settled themselves on the wrought-iron bench, Jared glanced over his shoulder to make sure they were well out of view. "I'm most obliged that you consented to see me, Hetty," he confessed.

"The pleasure is mine. All the girls at the academy think highly of you, Jared, although I don't mean to puff you up with such knowledge. You do seem to be a serious, strong-minded sort. There's some purpose to you. Not like some of the other boys who just want to take over their fathers' businesses or travel to faraway places."

"That's very nice of you to say," Jared said, a little startled by her forthright manner. He thought to himself, *I'll certainly not have to guess what she is thinking.*

"I like girls who speak their minds," Jared said. "Most, it seems to me, do a good bit of giggling and whispering and hiding behind their fans."

"Not I," Hetty said firmly. "Someday I hope to be just like Abigail Adams. Have you met her, Jared? She is not only a woman but a person as well. I can't figure out why Father sends me for schooling if all I'm to do is marry a man and keep my thoughts to myself. There doesn't seem any point in that; wouldn't you agree?"

A cool breeze swept wisps of brown hair off her forehead. Jared edged closer to her but resisted the urge to place his hand around her shoulder.

A flush filled Hetty's cheeks. Clearing her throat, she jumped up and turned away. "Sounds like some commotion over there. Look, Jared, people seem to be gathering down the street." Climbing onto a nearby rock, Hetty removed a dainty pair of opera glasses from her purse and squinted as she tried to focus on what was happening.

"The Light Dragoons! They're getting into formation for the parade. Here, take a peek," she said getting down and handing the glasses to Jared. "The officers of Cincinnati are there as well, I think."

"You know," Jared said as he squinted his eyes for a better view, "those men are all old friends of General Washington's, many of them from the war. This should be quite a reunion day for the general."

"How do you know so much, Jared—about the war, I mean? Studying you from afar, it would seem your entire life has been spent mastering English and practical mathematics. My father is forever saying to my brothers that if they took their studies one-half as seriously as you do, they might make something of themselves."

Jared could hardly believe that his name had actually been mentioned in the Morris home, let alone in such respectable terms.

"Well," he answered, "because of Uncle Thomas's position as George Washington's aide during the war, he has spent many an evening detailing battle after battle for me. Elizabeth and Mary aren't terribly interested. And I suppose he has always wanted me to understand the effect the war has had on all of our lives. For my father's sake, I very much like to believe it was important. He never made it home from the Battle of Princeton."

Hetty didn't know what to say. In the middle of their awkward silence Jared wondered how he could have said what he did. What a first meeting: They started out in a cemetery and ended up talking about his dead father. He had never discussed his father with anyone—until this very moment—and it seemed right to bring it up.

The church tower bell struck two times.

"Hetty," Jared said frantically, "I must go. If we walk fast I can see you to your door. I wish it could have been longer—our visit, I mean."

"That's all right," she said, taking his arm. Although her gesture startled him, he relaxed as they hurried through the gate and down Fourth Street. Having Hetty by his side seemed like the most natural thing in the world.

"Perhaps we can meet next Sunday?" he said cautiously.

"Or even before," she answered eagerly. "I begin my drawing lessons with Charles Wilson Peale tomorrow. Most of my practice sketching will be done in the yard."

"Really!" Jared couldn't hide his excitement. "Well, then, I'll look for you this week."

Market Street was packed with horses, carriages, and people clamoring for the best view of the general. The citizens of Philadelphia had been readying themselves for weeks to give General Washington a proper welcome, and Jared began to see the impossibility of seeing Hetty to her home.

"I'd best leave you here," Hetty said, stopping on the corner of Fifth and Chestnut, "as Mother will probably be on the front stoop waiting to greet General Washington. Good day, Jared. I hope we'll see each other again soon." After a moment she disappeared into the crowd.

There was no time to dwell on feelings as Jared bolted into a run.

At the State House Gouverneur Morris greeted him impatiently. "Where *have* you been, Master Jared?" he shouted for all to hear.

CHAPTER TWO

"WHAT have you been up to, Master Mifflin?" Gouverneur Morris continued, further embarrassing Jared in front of the gathering dignitaries and making him feel guilty about his secret rendezvous. "Your uncle assured me of your services." His testy attitude made Jared grit his teeth.

Having counted on Gouverneur Morris's usual wit and good nature, Jared was now concerned that his tardiness would be reported to Uncle Thomas. He elbowed his way up the marble steps to the place where the governor was giving instructions—Jared hoped this aggressive behavior would demonstrate an eagerness to perform any chore the man had for him.

"Well, you're here. That's really all that matters," Gouverneur Morris said. "By my calculations, the general's entourage will arrive at half after the hour. We've no time to spare. Run inside and bring me two benches. We can't have the greeting committee passing out from the heat."

Jared darted inside the State House door; Joseph Fry, the official doorkeeper, held it open as Jared brought both benches on to the small portico. Mr. Fry's irritation about the mass confusion taking place on *his* doorstep was amusing. It was rare that anyone other than he control the comings and goings in his building. Jared tried to be pleasant, but Mr. Fry simply returned his amenities with a stony glance.

"Now then," Gouverneur Morris ordered as soon as the benches were in place, "go around back and find the large ladder. We'll need to drape these banners across here."

Jared returned, lugging the ladder and muddying his good jacket, just as Dr. Franklin was arriving.

"Clear the way, I say," Gouverneur Morris cried out, trying without success to maintain a semblance of order. "Make a path, you hear. Dr. Franklin arrives."

His cronies were stumbling about, making a feeble attempt at crowd control. Jared was trying to catch his breath after securing the mighty ladder in the mud and climbing to its top. From his new vantage point he could see the prisoners from the city jail gently setting Dr. Franklin's sedan chair directly in front of the State House. The crowd roared as a genteel-looking criminal opened the door and escorted the good doctor up the first steps to the bench Jared had moved into position minutes before. *The man must only be doing a short time for not paying his taxes, or some such minor offense,* Jared thought.

"Catch!" a voice shouted from the other side of the door frame. Jared looked over and spotted a young man about his age waiting to toss him a few hundred feet of bunting.

"Ready?" the boy asked, preparing to throw the mass he had cleverly bundled into a tight ball.

Jared nodded, steadying himself with his left hand and reaching out with his right. *God, don't let me fall,* he thought—*not in front of all these people and not on top of Dr. Franklin.* The doctor was now bending his neck backward, staring straight up at what Jared was doing. His broad smile enlarged his already huge face. Steadied by his cane, which he held between his legs, Dr. Franklin was characteristically enjoying the confusion as though he were sitting front row center in the theater.

Whump! The bunting flew through the air, unraveling in flight, part of it draping about Jared's body. The crowd roared.

"Hurry up, you two!" Gouverneur Morris shouted, pacing back and forth. By his appearance, he seemed certain that all would not be in place by the time General Washington's carriage reached Chestnut Street.

Jared hammered in two nails to secure the banner and scampered down the ladder, which he hid behind a convenient group of shrubs. The ever-increasing pitch of the crowd's cheering signaled to those in the greeting party that the procession had reached Arch and Second streets.

"Stand over there, on the bottom step, Jared," Gouverneur Morris barked impatiently, "and you, too," he said, pointing at the other boy.

"We'll not see a thing from here," Jared whispered to the boy.

"Not to fear," he answered in a thick English accent. "Once the coach arrives, you'll see the crowds surge forward. There'll be no controlling anyone. That's when we'll move to a better spot."

"How clever!" Jared said. "What brings you here to work? I've not seen you before."

"My name is William . . . William Ellsworth." He extended his hand. "I'm houseboy to Dr. Franklin."

"Dr. Franklin!" Jared said, amazed. "He's just about our most famous citizen. How did you manage a job with him?"

Before William could answer, the cannons began firing in salute. The din was both shocking and thrilling. But in the midst of the enthusiastic spectators, Jared stood emotionless. He didn't care much for the flourish and fluff of ceremony. Only one thing was on his mind—to finally get a glimpse of the man everyone considered *the* American hero.

After all, it was Washington for whom his father had gone off to battle.

Jared recollected that he hadn't really understood what was happening at the time. He remembered sitting under the big old oak tree as Father tried to explain why he had packed his rifle and clothes and was going away for a while. His father had repeated again and again that he was needed by a General Washington and how Washington had called for the aid of his countrymen.

"Uncle Thomas is working for General Washington," Father had said, "and now they need my help as well. Take care of your mother and your sisters, Jared. And, son, I have something for you." He had pulled a small book from his pocket, placing it into Jared's hand. "You'll find all the answers to the trouble that's going on right here in this little book. Keep it safe for me, and when I return we'll read it together."

Jared remembered being enveloped by his father's arms for the last time before he rode off down the dusty path. After he was gone, Jared had run to his room, where he hid the book under his pillow.

When the news came that his father had been killed in battle, Jared remembered going straight to his room without saying a word to anyone, without shedding a tear. He had taken the book from its secret place and had leafed through it with the hope of finding his father somewhere within its pages. In the middle a phrase had been underlined and written beside it, in the margin, were the words *"For Jared."* Although he was just learning to read and write, he had copied the phrase word for word in his slow and careful scrawl until he fell asleep on the floor beside his writings:

> These are the times that try men's souls. . . .
> Those who expect to reap the blessings of
> freedom must, like men, undergo the fatigue
> of supporting it.

Jared continued to cling to these words during times of trouble. Tragically, he found they again brought him comfort when he lost his sisters and mother to the fever of 1777.

Now, ten years later, Jared was about to come face to face with the man who inspired his father to go off forever.

The general alighted from his carriage, Uncle Thomas not far behind him. Tall and stately, he had a serious air about him that Jared noticed at once. He didn't seem very outgoing. However, his manner was such that each person in the crowd felt he or she was being greeted personally with a wave or a smile. Jared was struck by his deep-set eyes—they seemed to pierce through and beyond the tumultuous welcome. As he moved regally up the State House steps, he shook hands, listened carefully to greetings, and then stood erect— almost at attention—as the ceremony continued. Jared thought the general seemed almost embarrassed by all the fuss, eager instead to get on with what he had come for. He tried to picture how George Washington must have performed in battle and found the image came easily. Perhaps this man really was the great American hero.

"Jared!" William said. "Hey, Jared, are you all right?"

"What?" Jared answered. The present came slowly into focus.

"The ceremonies . . . they're over," William said. "I must be off with Dr. Franklin now. It was nice working with you, old boy."

"The pleasure was mine," Jared said somewhat uncertainly. He watched as Dr. Franklin's sedan chair was carried through the crowd and around the corner.

"Jared, over here." Uncle Thomas motioned to him. It was hard not to notice him—built like Jared's father, Thomas Mifflin towered among others in any crowd. "We're walking the general to the Morris mansion. Come along."

"The Morrises," Jared said, trying to sound casual. With his hand he covered the beginning of a smile that he preferred not to share, while a voice inside his head shouted, *We're going to Hetty's house!*

Guiding him by the arm, Uncle Thomas led the general through the cheering throngs. Jared followed obediently behind as they crossed the Commons and headed toward Market Street.

A large group had already gathered by the Morris home—onlookers hoping to catch a glimpse of the general. Jared could see Hetty standing on the porch with Mr. and Mrs. Morris as they approached the house. He was determined to get as close to her as possible. Remembering William's advice on maneuvering in and around crowds, Jared inched his way through the commoners, saying, "Excuse me," several times in a most official tone of voice, until he was standing just to the right of the stoop. Hetty noticed him and began to edge over in his direction as Robert Morris officially welcomed the general to his "home for the summer."

"You must be in need of some tea and relaxation after your long journey," Mrs. Morris added. At that the front door was swept open and Hetty's parents escorted General Washington and Uncle Thomas inside. It was clear; no one else was invited. Hetty turned and nodded to Jared. Then she, too, disappeared into the house.

That recognition alone left Jared breathless. He turned on his heels and walked up Market Street, jauntily tipping his hat to whomever he passed. He gave two beggars a few pence and looked around for a hawker so he could buy himself a sweet. Famished, he was happy to be heading home from a long day of total exhilaration.

He entered the house through the entrance to the kitchen, where he hoped to find Margaret, the Mifflin house servant.

"Is there anything to eat?" he inquired. He watched her remove a pot from the boiling-hot hearth.

"I've just put up a batch of strawberry tarts that might suit your fancy, master. But I wouldn't want you to spoil your appetite. There's a hog roasting on the spit. I'll be serving it up with all the trimmings."

"Now that sounds good!" Grabbing several tarts and a few scones left over from breakfast, Jared headed for his room. He stripped to the waist and flopped upon his bed. Usually the muggy days made him lethargic, but today he simply felt light.

Hetty. Hetty. Hetty. Her name glided in and out of his thoughts. It was unbelievable that she should actually turn out to be as wonderful as he had imagined.

That night Jared tossed and turned in his bed, the sheet barely draped across his body. It had been an emotional day. Being with Hetty felt so warm and good, and seeing George Washington added insight into the events of his past. He was finally going to find out about the life his father had lived and the beliefs for which he died.

Cigar smoke wound its way up the circular staircase, cloaking his room with the heavy aroma of several kinds of tobacco. *Ah yes,* Jared thought, *Uncle Thomas is entertaining again.* These evening meetings were becoming nightly occurrences as the Constitutional Convention drew near. Old Uncle Thomas certainly was doing everything in his power to guide the Pennsylvania delegation into making decisions about what they hoped to gain from the Convention.

Jared puffed up his pillow and put his hands behind his head. The framed cross-stitch that hung on the wall opposite his bed caught his eye. Aunt Sarah had made it for him as a commencement gift. Even in the dark he could read the words perfectly:

> These are the times that try men's souls. . . .
> Those who expect to reap the blessings of
> freedom must, like men, undergo the fatigue
> of supporting it.

He found himself thinking that perhaps the battle of which Thomas Paine wrote did not only apply to the Revolutionary War or physical struggle. As he listened night after night to Uncle Thomas and his colleagues, it became clear to him that the nation was gearing up for its second great battle.

According to his uncle, the soul of the country was crumbling. He said that George Washington would not have made the trip to Philadelphia if he didn't believe it to be so. And if the colonies expected to "reap the blessings" of further freedoms, it seemed that the men coming to Philadelphia were going to have to "undergo fatigue" reaching a consensus. Jared fell off to sleep with an odd sense of excitement about living in Philadelphia at such a time.

Perhaps he would be part of this second great battle. Perhaps he could make a contribution, just as his father had before him.

"Jared, Jared, get yourself up!" Annie was saying. She nudged his shoulders with uncertainty in an effort to awaken him. "Your uncle wants you down to breakfast immediately."

"Morning," Jared mumbled, "already! What did you say, Annie?"

She was busily taking garments out of his dresser and placing them on the bed. "Your uncle is already taking his morning meal. He told me to have you wear your best finery and to hurry."

Jared yawned. "There's no more school and yesterday was Sunday. Why the ruffles and jacket and all those layers?" he asked sleepily. A morning breeze drifted through the window and with it a small parade of flies. It was going to be hotter than the day before. Jared fell back onto his bed and pulled the softly worn down pillow over his head.

"Now, now, Master Jared, none of that. I'll be back," she said. From the staircase that led to the kitchen, he heard her call, "You know your uncle. When he has a request you'd best carry it out."

As he buttoned his breeches, Jared couldn't fathom what the fuss was all about. He wasn't quite sure that he wanted to find out, either. Annie had left a basin of cool water on the washstand. He sprinkled his face and hands and patted them dry. By the time he returned from the privy pit out back he was beginning to feel nearly awake. With a last-minute tug at his clothes Jared appeared at the dining room door.

"Good morning," Uncle Thomas said, greeting him with a mouth full of scone. As usual, the *Pennsylvania Gazette* and two other periodicals lay next to his plate. But curiously enough, Uncle was not buried behind any of them. Instead, his eyes peered over his spectacles as he said, "Jared, my boy, I've been thinking for months how best we could put your talents to work this summer, and I think I've come up with just the right opportunity."

Margaret appeared with a hot plate of sausage and eggs. Jared could feel Uncle Thomas gearing up for one of his longer monologues. He couldn't help but think that his uncle had already planned exactly which direction this conversation would go. Rarely did you actually converse with Thomas Mifflin. Mainly you listened, nodded, and answered a question or two near the end of his discourse—if, that is, he felt compelled to hear your opinion.

So, Jared decided to concentrate on his eggs and simply wait until the conversation ran its course.

"It was brought to my attention last night by Messieurs Ingersoll and Fitzsimmons that James Madison is in a most disagreeable state because the Convention has been delayed," Uncle Thomas began.

Jared stopped munching on Margaret's freshly baked bread, wondering what, if anything, this had to do with him. It couldn't be that Uncle had roused him out of bed simply to air his latest thoughts on the outcome of the country. If this was the only agenda for Jared's early rising, he knew he would find it hard to keep from losing his patience.

"As some of my colleagues began to discuss Mr. Madison's state of mind," Uncle Thomas continued, "it occurred to us that the man is simply overworked. For months he's been working on this Convention almost single-handedly."

Jared simply nodded.

"Each day, your Aunt Sarah reports his every move as told to her by Mrs. House. The man works from dawn to dusk, living in solitary, save for Joseph Fry, who assists him when he's not watching the State House door."

Jared opened his mouth to ask a question, but his uncle cut him off. "Now I for one, being Chairman of the State Assembly, know that Joseph Fry is a nice sort of fellow but practically useless, if you know what I mean," Uncle Thomas said as he continued his one-way conversation. He barely looked up from his plate as he continued to shovel food onto the fork with his knife. "In any event, we all decided last night that Madison's mood would be substantially improved if he had an assistant . . . someone who could be trusted to run important errands, take care of details, buy supplies . . . that sort of thing. Of course, it should be a person who is smart and able, and that someone, Jared, we've all concluded, should be you!"

Jared choked on his bread. He had almost lost track of the conversation when he heard the word "you."

"Me?" Jared garbled. "Well, sir, I simply don't—"

"Now, now, I'll have no excuses, none at all. Finish up your tea, my boy—we're off to pay a visit to Mr. Madison."

Jared's stomach suddenly felt most disagreeable; his mind raced. James Madison! Besides George Washington and Dr. Franklin, Mr. Madison was the most discussed politician at school. Work for James Madison! The entire idea seemed preposterous.

"Come along, my boy," Uncle called from the back doorway. "We want to engage Madison before his mind is engrossed in matters of state."

Market Street was already crowded with Monday morning farmers who had come to town to sell their vegetables, livestock, and all manner of goods. Temporary stands were being erected wherever there was a free spot. Some people sold their goods right from carts. Jared and Uncle Thomas found themselves trailing behind a broom seller. His basket—perched upon his shoulders—was steeped high with all shapes and sizes of brooms.

"We can't even see where we are going," Uncle Thomas said agitatedly. He stepped up his pace to pass the young merchant, but in his haste he stumbled over a basket of fish that a fishmonger had just set down on the cobblestone street.

"Damn it," Uncle whispered under his breath. "Why don't they keep their smelly fish by the docks?"

Their pace renewed, they rushed past two Indians, one of whom was dressed in the manner of a Cherokee chief.

"I'll bet he's in town hoping to meet the delegates," Uncle Thomas told Jared. "We've heard the Indians want mention of their needs in the Constitution."

Market Street was like a grand show on market days. Knife grinders, glassblowers, milkmaids, lantern makers, and merchants with freshly imported European goods were everywhere. Jared loved to stand around and see who was the best bargainer. Commoners and house servants were brilliant at the game.

He had forgotten for the moment what lay ahead, when he heard his uncle say, "C'mon boy, you *are* dragging your feet today."

Once his nervousness subsided, Jared found himself wondering— not for the first time—why he let his uncle push him into these situations. It was so difficult to put up a struggle, especially because the Mifflins treated him like their natural-born son. They availed him of every possible opportunity a young man could want or need. Jared said to himself with a mental shrug of his shoulders, *I have to admit, life with Uncle Thomas has never been dull.*

Uncle Thomas slapped Jared's back in encouragement and pulled open the heavy State House door. Regardless of the many times Jared had been dragged off to one session or another in this place, today it had an eerie feeling. He had heard so much about this man—even studied some of his writings in school. He seemed larger than life. . . . As a result, it was quite a shock when Uncle Thomas marched through the large green door leading into the East Room, booming, "Good day, James," and Jared gazed upon a short man. As he rose to greet them, Jared calculated that James Madison couldn't be more than five feet three! However, his well-proportioned body was un-usually muscular and his complexion ruddy. James Madison stood tall; he looked like a man who could guide a nation.

"Quite a day yesterday, aye, James?" Uncle Thomas volunteered. "Now that the good general is here, it seems all is in place."

Jared's uncle waited for a response, and when there was none he continued, "Washington paid a call on Dr. Franklin last evening, and they both agreed the time is now or never for a Constitution."

"I wish that were so," Mr. Madison said, finally responding to their presence. "We have the leading characters, as it were, but we are lacking a necessary quorum. I am most concerned that after

The bustle of Market Street, viewed from outside the open market

pleading with Washington to grace us with his attendance we shall lose his presence if the others fail to arrive shortly."

"Not to fear," Uncle Thomas said lightly. "I hear John Blair and George Wythe are on their way from Virginia, and the Charleston is due in from South Carolina any day now. Rutledge and his delegation should be aboard. In the meantime, I have come on official business. Meet my nephew, Master Jared Mifflin."

So I'm official business now, Jared thought as he crossed the room and firmly met Mr. Madison's handshake. There followed an awkward moment of silence which, to Jared's relief, was broken by Uncle Thomas.

"I'd like to take the liberty of offering you Jared's services. He is a bright boy, possessing a serious nature. It was the feeling of my colleagues here in Pennsylvania that you should have an aide at your disposal, prior to and during this most tedious Convention."

"I must confess," Mr. Madison said, gazing at the piles of papers and books that surrounded him, "that there is still much to be accomplished and a helper would, indeed, be welcome. Master Jared—" he eyed him up and down now very carefully—"do you feel up to the task of long hours, working some nights, and Saturdays as well?"

Jared turned to his uncle and back to Mr. Madison. Though he was a bit surprised at such a rigorous schedule, he quickly assured the man of his willingness. At that moment, he wasn't exactly sure why he should be eager for such a job, but he instinctively knew this was an opportunity not to be passed up.

"I'm not certain where the funds will come from to pay you, my boy," Mr. Madison said. "The Convention is presently running without a budget."

No salary! Jared thought. *True, this might well be an experience of a lifetime, but I'm in need of money for summer outings and university expenses.*

"Not to worry," Uncle said to both of them, clearing his throat, which was something he always did when he was stalling for time. "Our delegation, being your hosts, is right now making plans for various expenses." Jared was unconvinced by his uncle's tact, but remained silent. "This should be no problem, no problem at all. So, shall we consider it all as settled?"

"I should think so," Mr. Madison said. "I would be a fool to turn down such an offer. I will see you tomorrow then, Master Jared." He rose and leaned over the desk to shake Jared's hand.

Aware that Mr. Madison was anxious to get back to work, Uncle Thomas and Jared took their leave.

"I'm late for my next appointment," Uncle Thomas announced, pushing the front door open while glancing at his pocket watch.

"But I have a million questions for you," Jared said in desperation.

"Do I detect some apprehension?" Uncle Thomas asked, his arm blanketing his nephew's shoulder.

"Well, I would like to know a bit more about the man."

"You were everyone's choice for the position, my boy. Now, no more questions. Mr. Madison is a fine judge of character. You heard his sense of relief at having the services of an intelligent local lad. It'll all work out fine, you'll see."

"But why did he come to Philadelphia so much earlier than anyone else? Is he trying to take control of the country?"

"No, no, nothing of the sort. For one, he's a bachelor and doesn't have the family constraints many of us have. And besides, the Convention was really his idea. Do you remember when I went to Annapolis last year?"

Jared nodded.

"Well, it was James Madison who had the foresight to call us all together to propose a Constitutional Convention. He really is quite remarkable—possessing an eagerness and fervor like no other man I've met. If we leave him to his own resources I have no doubts that he'll get precisely what he wants out of the delegates. You mark my words. For a man of thirty-five, he knows almost as much about the political process as old Ben Franklin."

Jared was impressed.

"I'll be off to the docks now. A shipment of rum was due in this morning. Tell Aunt Sarah I shall be taking supper at the City Tavern with Captain Smith. It will take some doing to get the price I want. Oh, and you had better stop by the tailor for new breeches and shirts. We can't have you looking tattered when you report for work."

Well, Jared figured as he meandered down Second Street, *I think I'm in for the summer of my life!*

CHAPTER THREE

"TWO o'clock and all is well," chanted the night watchman as he passed outside Jared's open window.

Jared had gone to bed early in anticipation of his first day on the job. But he was not able to settle into sleep. He had heard the watchman's hourly weather and time announcements since ten o'clock and was still wide-awake when the lamplighter replaced the wick in the streetlight in front of the house.

Enough of this tossing and turning, he thought finally. Getting out of bed, Jared relit his candle and grabbed Oliver Goldsmith's latest book. *If all else fails, surely* Deserted Village *will put me to sleep.* His concentration was broken by two drunken sailors careening down the street. The dreadful chantey they sang broke harshly through the heaviness of night. Jared put his book down upon his chest and wondered what it must be like to sail the seas, to see different ports around the world. . . .

Only four hours after he drifted off to sleep Jared was awakened by Annie. Although the proper working day for gentlemen in Philadelphia began at ten o'clock, Jared knew that Mr. Madison had been arriving at the State House well before nine. He timed his arrival and appeared on the State House steps at five minutes after nine o'clock. Pulling hard on the mighty brass door handle, he walked into the grand hallway. The buttoning of his jacket kept Jared's nervous hands busy while his eyes adjusted to the darkness.

Another quiet day? How strange, Jared thought. *This place is always busy with a trial or a hearing or something.*

A mouse squeaked across the floor, disappearing into a hole in the wall.

I'll feel like disappearing as well, Jared said to himself, *if Mr. Madison isn't here yet.* He approached the half-open door quietly and was about to walk in when a voice came from the darkness: "May I help you?"

Startled to find someone lurking about, Jared's body stiffened.

"I'm Joseph Fry, the doorkeeper. Do you have formal business here, young man, or are you just snooping about?"

"I'm to meet Mr. James Madison," Jared stammered. "He expected me at nine o'clock. Is he here?"

"Yes, yes, of course he is," Joseph Fry said with an air of authority. "I shall have to announce you. Follow me."

And with that they walked straight into the East Room. Jared felt smug when Mr. Madison confirmed that he indeed was expecting young Master Mifflin.

"Thank you, Mr. Fry," he said. "That will be all." The tone of his voice dismissed Mr. Fry without further discussion.

"Good day, sir," Jared said brightly, clearing his throat as the words came out in a rather uncontrolled high pitch. Sometimes when he was nervous his voice played tricks on him.

"Sit down, sit down, my boy," Mr. Madison said, motioning grandly. His desk had been pushed over beside one of the large windows, and he was practically hidden behind a stack of books. "My, my, you are the punctual one. I just heard the tower bell chime. Good. Good. Good. I like that quality in people; I wish some of the delegates were as diligent."

"I'm afraid the weather hasn't helped much, sir," Jared responded.

"What's that?" Mr. Madison asked, peering over the top of his spectacles.

"The awful weather. We've had such a rainy season that the rivers are swollen, and my uncle says the country roads are barely passable. With trees falling across back lanes and blocking passage, many stage lines are way off schedule."

"Well, be that as it may, we can't spend the day worrying about travel conditions, can we? Come, pull up a chair. I've been working on a possible seating arrangement. Let me assure you that these delegates are all sensitive—those from the big colonies think they should sit in the front row, and those from the smaller colonies will have their feelings hurt if they think for a moment that they smell a monopoly of power. It's going to be an awful dilemma, really, keeping the entire lot of them content."

Jared had never thought about size causing discord among the colonies.

"Now, Jared, one of your daily tasks will be to keep track of arrivals. As soon as we have equal representation from all the states we can begin this Convention."

"I see, sir, but you are expecting more than thirteen persons, are you not? I mean, in my uncle's group alone there are at least seven men who plan to attend."

"Oh, indeed," Mr. Madison responded. "We, that is those of us who attended the Annapolis Convention, invited each of the thirteen colonies to send several representatives. John Dickenson, who received the replies, informs me that our group should number fifty-five in all. Unfortunately, various pressures will delay the arrival of several until well into June. As far as I'm concerned, we should begin when there are representatives from seven colonies. Now, here is a list of those expected," Mr. Madison said as he passed a crumbled piece of parchment to Jared. "I want you to make daily rounds to the boarding houses where gentlemen would stay—assuming you know the places."

"Indeed, sir," Jared said, trying to sound like Mr. Madison.

"There's the City Tavern, the London Coffee House . . ." he began to keep track on his fingers . . . "the Half Moon, the Indian Queen, where you board, Mrs. House's, and—"

"Enough, my boy. These are the details of which I hope to clear my head now that you are working for me."

"Yes, sir! And other jobs? What else would you have me do?"

"As I look around the room, I'm finding inkwells empty. We shall need all manner of writing supplies: pens, powder, parchment, paper—you know, those sort of items. Let me see, what else?" he said, stalling while searching for another one of his lists amidst the clutter.

"Ah, yes, here it is. I worked on it last evening. Now let me see . . . presently, there aren't enough chairs. Can you locate a few more?" Jared was puzzled; he'd never had cause to think of furniture before.

James Madison continued to read his list. "I presume most of the delegates will have the presence of mind to bring along their portable writing tables. However, if not, we shall need plenty of ledgers. Leaning on these tables will only tear the precious paper as pen hits surface."

He certainly is a man of detail, Jared thought to himself. *I wouldn't have considered one-half of these things!*

Mr. Madison went on: "The room will be dark. We shall need plenty of candles and additional holders, of course."

"But sir, the daylight lasts late into the evening during the summer."

"I know. I know," Mr. Madison retorted, rather agitated. "But it is my hope to keep these proceedings absolutely secret. If the others agree, we shall be closing up the windows and drawing the shutters."

"Well, if that's the case," Jared suggested, "I'd best purchase fans for everyone, because you will suffocate without a breeze or a breath of fresh air."

"Good point," Mr. Madison agreed, adding fans to his list. "I like you, Jared, you can think on your feet; and get some flyswatters.

This place is full of those nasty little things—they've been driving me crazy." Unconsciously, he reached down to scratch his leg. "Now to continue with the list—" Jared sensed that Mr. Madison was getting bored with all the trivia and wanted to get back to work—"get us some pottery jugs for water, and order a daily water delivery while you're at it. We'll need ashtrays and more pipe holders, a few extra bells to quell the squabbles, a few more spittoons . . . and the rest should be self-explanatory."

The tower bell chimed half after ten. "Be off now, Master Jared, so I might get back to my business. I am very grateful to have you aboard," he said, rising to his feet and escorting Jared out.

"Thank you, sir. Oh, one more thing—whom shall I tell the merchants to bill?"

"Ah, yes. I suppose we should use your uncle's advice. Tell them Robert Morris and his men are to be charged for the expenses. When I take supper there this evening I shall pose the problem. And if the merchants question you further, tell them the government is paying." He laughed. "How funny that is! I wonder how many realize that at present there is no government, that the colonies are all acting like independent countries."

Jared was beginning to understand the urgency of the Constitutional Convention. "I hadn't realized, Mr. Madison. It makes me feel honored to be of service to you. I'll be off now," he said, stuffing the various lists into his waistcoat pocket. "I'll see you at day's end with a progress report," Jared called back to Mr. Madison from the hallway.

He felt relief as the fresh air and daylight hit his face. The State House was only going to get more stuffy as the summer wore on. *But never mind,* Jared found himself thinking. Something told him that in a small way he was being given a chance to serve his country. His father would have been proud of him today. And he had to admit that he felt pretty good himself.

Jared sat on the stoop to figure out an efficient way in which to accomplish everything. He knew if he planned carefully, he could design a circuitous route that would bring him back to the State House at the end of each day.

"Jared! Jared Mifflin, is that you?"

Jared looked up. He saw Jonathan Freeman meandering across the yard, cricket bat swinging from his hand and looking as though he hadn't a care in the world. *Probably doesn't either,* Jared thought.

"What are you up to? We stopped by your house on the way to practice, but you weren't home."

"I've gotten myself a job," Jared admitted rather timidly.

"A job!" Jonathan snapped back. "But why?"

"Well, actually, Uncle Thomas got me a job," Jared continued, feeling embarrassed about not being more in control of his own life. "I'm working all summer for James Madison. Or at least until the Constitutional Convention is over."

"Madison. *The* James Madison?"

"Yep." Jared felt a bit better after hearing Jonathan's reaction. "It all happened so fast. I'm afraid the lazy plans we had will elude me. Unless, of course, the cricket matches could be scheduled after working hours."

"But Jared, what happened to our pact—a summer of exploring, of wine, women, and fox hunts—some fun before university."

Jared felt a pang of jealousy. Of course, there was Hetty; Jonathan didn't know that.

"Not for me, at least for the time being."

"Well, I must admit, you've gotten yourself into a pretty impressive mess," Jonathan said. "You've always been more determined than the rest of us. As I looked over all of our friends at commencement, I figured that you, if anyone, would be the one to go on to the Continental Congress. Guess I was right," he said, strolling off and shaking his head. "Ebin, Edward, and I won't let you work all the time. We can't have you turning dull on us, Jared. We'll be 'round, you'll see," he said as he disappeared around the corner.

Jared headed off toward the Indian Queen. He was delighted at having an excuse to visit the various taverns about town. The stained glass windows and doors that seemed typically to adorn most taverns further darkened their interiors, creating a mysterious air even on the brightest of days. It was in these surroundings that the rich mixed with the poor; travelers from across the sea filled the conversation with foreign accents. Sea captains sold their goods, and the smell of good food and drink permeated the air.

Business meetings were carried on behind heavy woven curtains, which could be drawn around the eating booths. The innkeepers were always throwing someone out on the street for rowdy behavior. And it was not uncommon to see a man being chased up the street by a barmaid offended by his advances.

Nearing the corner of Fourth and Chestnut, Jared watched as a group of men who were departing the Indian Queen stopped in mid-stride. Anticipating action, he quickened his pace, and as he approached the now-silent group, he heard what they had—the sound of a horse whinnying and a raised voice above the general commotion. Trouble seemed to be brewing in the stable area. Jared followed the curious spectators down the alley that adjoined the tavern and led to the stables.

"When I ask for my horse to be saddled and ready by midmorning, I don't expect a delay," shouted a rather brash young man, fashionably clothed in an expensive-looking brown jacket and matching breeches, with a leather whip tucked neatly under his arm. Throughout his tirade he paced impatiently in a manner that was almost childlike.

Jared studied his face. *He looks familiar, but such behavior generally does not accompany the people that move in Mifflin circles*, he thought.

Meanwhile, three other men awaited their horses. The lone dark-skinned livery boy was working as fast as possible, but not fast enough for the angry man.

"I mean it!" the man said, elbowing past the onlookers. Drawing his whip, he gave the cobblestone wall of the alley a lashing as he approached the boy.

"You're all worthless," he shouted, referring—Jared assumed— to his dark skin. Terrified that the whip was going to come down on his back, the boy froze, his eyes burning from unshed tears. His inaction only served to further anger the man who, upon reaching the livery boy, shoved him to the ground with such force that he landed across the stable yard by Jared's feet.

"Give me my horse! I'll finish the job," the man continued abusively. "I shall certainly expect better service from you during this long summer," he said as he fastened the last buckle on the saddle. He spit a mouthful of tobacco in the direction of the boy, narrowly missing his own spotlessly polished boots.

At that moment an older gentleman came rushing out of the tavern's back door, shaking his walking stick and shouting, "You can't treat my boy that way, Dayton!"

"Dayton!" Jared whispered under his breath. *That's who he is. Of all people.* Uncle Thomas had mentioned his name to Jared on numerous occasions, telling him to watch Jona Dayton's progress as he promised to be a great politician some day.

"You had best find yourself another hostelry, Dayton," the old man said. "I shall find it impossible to dine and board in the same place as you."

"What's the matter with you, Baldwin?" Jona Dayton said sarcastically as he mounted his horse. "You're the one who comes from slave country. I'd think you'd know how to treat these Negroes. They respond best to whips and orders. Giddap," he ordered his animal. And with that he sped down the alley, leaving behind a trail of dust and a murmuring crowd.

Jared reached down and gave the stable boy his hand, helping to brush the dirt and hay off his new uniform. The boy then hurried off to finish saddling the waiting horses.

"Henry, pay him no mind," Abraham Baldwin said. "I shall talk to the innkeeper so that this sort of embarrassment does not occur again."

"Thank you, Mistuh Baldwin," Henry answered, still a bit shaken but determined to hold his head high.

As the spectators dispersed, Jared approached Henry. "I'm Jared

Mifflin. Pleased to meet you," he said extending his hand. Henry wasn't sure what Jared wanted and just gave him a nod before going back to his work. Jared watched the young man run back and forth between the stable and the horses, grabbing bridles, stirrups, and saddles for the remaining guests who had waited patiently during the unfortunate scene that had just transpired.

"You new here?" Jared asked. "I mean, are you from Philadelphia or did you come off a ship?" He was curious about whether Henry was a slave.

Because Jared continued to pursue him Henry decided to answer.

"My name's Henry Blair," he said cautiously. "I come with Mistuh Baldwin. We from Georgia. He's here on business—somethin' to do with the law, he says. After helpin' him on the long journey, he gave me permission to get a job. I'm chief livery boy here," he concluded with pride.

Jared was taken aback by the clarity with which Henry talked. Most blacks he knew had no formal education and spoke in an almost foreign tongue.

"I am surprised at Mr. Dayton," Jared volunteered. "He is supposed to be an up-and-coming political leader. He doesn't seem so up-and-coming, does he?"

The two boys looked at each other. For the first time Henry seemed to relax, and even managed a smile.

"Well, you learn something new every day—that is, if you keep your eyes open," Jared said. "That's what my uncle tells me anyway."

"Sure do," Henry agreed. "I do right here in this stable. Back home my family works for the Baldwins. We know what they want, what they 'spect for certain things; and we got us a house, garden, food, and some schoolin', too. Yessuh, Mistuh Baldwin's sistuh is teachin' me to read and write."

"Do you belong to them?" Jared asked. "I mean are you . . . a slave?"

"Yessuh," Henry admitted, "but it's not like you think. It's work—we just don't get money for it. Up here now, I get wages. If I like it bettuh I might just stay."

Henry gave the last horse a pat on its withers and said, "I best be gettin' on to my other chores. The stables need a cleanin', and I got to get me some hay down on Market Street."

Jared suddenly realized that he was working, too. "I must be off as well. Perhaps we can talk again sometime under better circumstances. One of my duties is to come 'round each day and check with the innkeepers to see which delegates have arrived. I now know that one from Georgia is here." Jared smiled and turned toward the tavern's back door.

He paused for a moment so that his eyes could adjust to the darkness within the windowless corridor. Linen skirts and muslin petticoats brushed against Jared as passing servant girls carried piles of cloth and bedding and trays of dishes to and from the grand staircase that was directly inside the front door. As the busy hallway became clearer his eyes rested upon a harried-looking elderly gentleman. Jared guessed that he was Mr. Thompson, the proprietor, if for no other reason than that he was dressed in a maroon waistcoat which matched in color the costumes of the other workers.

Jared approached the man just as he was directing a group of eight men into the main dining room. There seemed to be an inordinate amount of noonday traffic, which made him hesitate a moment before disturbing Mr. Thompson. *But chaos or not*, Jared thought, *I have a job to do.*

"Mr. Thompson, I presume?" he said sheepishly.

"I am, indeed," the man answered as he proceeded to once again seat himself on the high stool that stood behind an upright mahogany desk. "May I help you?"

"I hope so, sir," Jared said. "I am at the service of James Madison. It is his desire to know how many delegates to the Constitutional Convention you expect to board and which ones, aside from Mr. Dayton and Mr. Baldwin, have already arrived."

"As you can see, I've not the time to check my register just now, young man, but if you care to return in a few hours, I would be most happy to oblige."

"Thank you, sir. I shall stop back about three o'clock."

Heading out the front door, Jared pulled out his list. *This might be a perfect time to order the water deliveries and to stop off at the potters*, he thought. He decided to keep his eye out for vendors selling fans and flyswatters on the way. Fortunately, he was carrying enough currency to cover the smaller items on the list.

Before getting sidetracked by merchants, Jared stopped at Mrs. House's boardinghouse. He knew that she wasn't in the habit of serving her guests noon meals, and was certain that it would be a convenient time to confer with her regarding any new arrivals.

Mrs. House was eager to inform him that all of the most important visitors were already lodged in her quarters, save for General Washington. He jotted down the seven names she gave him and left as quickly as propriety would allow.

The next three hours soared by. Jared headed back to the Indian Queen, looking like a veritable hawker with a burlap bag filled with flyswatters and pitchers, slung over his shoulder, and twenty fans tied together dangling from his waist.

"Good afternoon, Mr. Thompson," Jared said, arriving promptly at three. "Your establishment certainly has quieted down," he ventured, attempting a bit of small talk.

"Oh, yes, yes indeed," the old man chuckled. "Fill up their bellies with good food and moisten their lips with a pint or two of ale and most of my guests take to their quarters for a midday snooze."

He was shuffling through a mound of papers on his desk. "Now then, lad, take out your pencil, and I'll tell you who has arrived and whom I expect in the next day or two."

Jared quickly situated himself on a nearby bench, grabbed his ledger, and started writing.

"We have here a Mr. Rufus King from Massachusetts, is he one?"

Jared nodded.

"How about William Huston from New Jersey, and let's see," he continued, running his fingers up and down the columns, "George Reade from Delaware. He seems to be arriving by ferry. It's way off schedule, as I understand it. Other chambers have been reserved for Mr. George Mason of New York. He's to be in number nine. Number twelve will be occupied by Hugh Williamson of North Carolina, and next to him will be John Langdon of New Hampshire. Can't count on him getting here for a while, as I hear they've been hit with torrential rains up north. I expect others will just appear at my doorstep without previous reservation," he continued, closing his book. "I'll let you know, my boy."

The State House clock chimed four just as Jared stepped out of the Indian Queen. He sped across the mall, eager to deliver this information to his new employer. *It will make him feel better—I hope he hasn't left yet,* Jared thought, and he quickened his pace. Under the weight of his large frame, his long legs felt heavy. It had been a hectic day, and tomorrow promised to be even more so.

CHAPTER FOUR

15th May
Early morning

*D*EAR *Hetty,*
    So much has happened since our meeting on Sunday. General Washington's arrival has brought a flourish of activity that I now believe will not stop until this Constitution is written. I can only imagine how your house is bustling with his comings and goings.

    I shall be most interested to hear your impressions of him, not only because he seems to be our most admired citizen, but also because I will be working for the Convention! James Madison has hired me as his aide. My position permits me free run of the city and flexible working hours.

    If you are in agreement, it would be most pleasing to meet you on occasion, perhaps when you are sketching on the Commons or out doing other errands.

    Since our meetings are best kept secret for now, I have an idea about how to arrange them. Should a day be suitable, stand by your front window when I pass by in the morning at nine o'clock. When you see me, indicate a rendezvous time by holding up so many fingers. If you do not appear, I shall know that a meeting that day is not convenient.

    I look forward to your answer tomorrow or the next day.
                    Very truly and respectfully,
                    I am your obedient servant, Jared

Armed with Hetty's letter, Jared couldn't get out of the house soon enough. As it was not a market day, the street was quiet and the footways clear of all confusion. Jared felt exhilarated as he swiftly walked the four blocks to Sixth and Market. His heart pounded as he scooted up to the front door of the Morrises' house, slipped the letter through the brass mail slot, and darted around the corner. *Phew*, he sighed, leaning against a brick wall. *I made it. Imagine if the butler had heard and opened the door before I escaped.*

Turning left on Chestnut, he headed to the docks, taking a shortcut through Strawberry Alley. *I may as well make an adventure out of this job*, Jared mused. Ordinarily, young men of his stature were not to go to such earthy places.

John Butler's stage to New York was bustling! Mr. Butler, Jared surmised from the tone of his voice, was frantic. Listening to the commotion, it seemed to Jared that Butler was one livery boy short, and to make matters worse, the coachman for his next trip had yet to appear. The scene attracted the attention of a buxom barmaid from the Bull's Head Tavern next door. She had long since stopped her sweeping and leaned on her broom at the top of the stoop until her employer discovered her standing idle.

"To work, you wench," the gruff tavern owner bellowed, slapping her on the fanny as he dumped garbage in the gutter. "'Tis a big day we have with two ships docking at any hour. This place will be full of mariners by noontime, y'hear?"

"Y' best treat a lady with dignity," she shouted back, taking her anger out on the footway, "or you shall have no one helping you when most y' need it."

Jared hurried by, nervous that he might be caught eavesdropping, and turned onto Water Street.

A cool breeze gave him relief from the already muggy air, even though it carried with it the odor of fish.

The dock area was astir—men building ships, others carting off goods, still others bargaining for merchandise. And then Jared spotted what he had been looking for: down to the left, at the far end of the dock was the *Canton*, the most mysterious of all ships. She, and only she, carried cargo to and from the Far East. The square-rigged mast and bright red hull made her stand out among the others.

As he continued walking toward her, he saw—gliding through the morning mist—another well-known vessel, the *Charming Polly*. Although smaller, she boasted a mermaidlike figurehead that gave her a special dignity all her own.

Jared wanted to find a place from which he could take in all the action. " 'Scuse me, master," a sailor boy said, rolling a giant barrel of rum down the cobblestone street to a waiting cart.

Jared worked his way around a group of men coiling line, and another man leaning up against a piling and strumming on his mandolin, seemingly without a care in the world. Jared spotted a group of large crates stacked on a deck at the Bridgewater Boat Works. Once atop a crate marked FRAGILE, he had a perfect view of the entire scene.

For years Uncle Thomas had been entertaining him with tales of the waterfront and of the sea captains that ruled it, but Jared was rarely permitted to frequent this area. "It's not the proper place for a young gentleman," Uncle Thomas would respond whenever Jared pleaded to accompany him.

His eyes came to rest on an energetic young man who appeared to be about Jared's age. He was talking and waving his arms in an animated fashion, first to one mariner, then another, and finally to the captain of the *Canton* himself. *He does look awfully familiar,* Jared thought, shielding his eyes from the sun and trying to place him. *Who the devil is he? . . . Well, I'll be—that's Dr. Franklin's houseboy,* he said with a slap of his thigh. *He certainly manages to be in all the exciting places,* Jared thought as he climbed down off the crate and headed toward him.

"Whatever are you up to, William Ellsworth?" Jared called out as he hastened down the crowded dock.

William turned, a bit startled that someone should know him. "I didn't think it proper for a gentleman, the likes of you, to be loitering about in such a common place," he answered by way of explanation.

"It is when he is in search of supplies for the Constitutional Convention. I was just passing through on my way to the pewterer over there," Jared countered, pointing his finger and wondering why he felt he had to justify being there at all. "And you, what business are you up to? I thought your duties revolved around caring for Dr. Franklin."

"Actually, I do whatever he needs of me. Today I am here to make certain that a highboy and a set of fine porcelain are carefully unloaded and safely delivered to the doctor's home."

Just then a husky voice bellowed from the hold. "Is there a Master Ellsworth topside?"

"Aye-aye, sir," William answered, sounding like part of the king's navy.

A weather-wrinkled face appeared out of the hatch. "It shall be another hour or so 'fore we see the Franklin cargo, laddy." And with that he disappeared.

"Well, so it goes," William said, shrugging his shoulders knowingly. "I should have expected as much. There are always delays in this shipping business. Would you like to stop off at the baker's and get something to eat?" he asked.

"I could use a bit of food in my stomach," Jared said, remembering he hadn't taken time for breakfast that morning. "How do you know so much about the shipping industry? When I spotted you there on the dock you looked as though you actually belonged."

"Well, one learns a lot crossing the Atlantic in one of these things," William answered, pointing to yet another vessel. "When I was orphaned back in London, I had the choice either to go to a workhouse or to stow away to America. I chose the latter with the hope that I could live with my uncle here. He's a farmer up in Massachusetts."

"Why aren't you there?" Jared probed, already fascinated with this wandering lad.

"Don't I wish I were," William said longingly, "but luck was working against me. The voyage over was without incident, and once here I had no trouble locating the farm. It is directly outside Boston. But alas," he sighed, "I did not find my uncle there. A neighbor told me that he and nearly one hundred other farmers were involved in some sort of revolt when their property was confiscated as a result of their being in debt. Some bloke named Daniel Shays led an attack on the courts—an actual battle I was told—and the farmers lost. Most are still in jail. Anyway," William continued in his upbeat manner, "with not a penny left to my name I was forced to find work that very day."

They had arrived at the baker's, and Jared, with stomach growling, insisted on buying. The two new friends leaned against the counter, munching on loaves of freshly baked bread, while William continued his story.

"The only job I could get was aboard a merchandise cart headed for Philadelphia. I'd heard reports that this city was the most prosperous in America. Now that I'm here, I suppose they were right."

"But working for Benjamin Franklin?" Jared asked, awe in his voice. "Besides General Washington, he's the country's leading citizen. Surely you didn't just knock on his door and ask for a job!"

William chuckled. "Of course not. But I did hear that a Dr. Franklin was looking to hire a houseboy. Not knowing who he was, I didn't for one minute fear the meeting, as others might have."

As he listened, Jared thought back on his experience with Mr. Madison the day before. He'd had such trepidation about meeting the man.

"And I later found out from George, Dr. Franklin's manservant, that he had hired me because I reminded the good doctor of himself when he was young."

"How's that?" Jared asked.

"Well, evidently he was a boy of humble means and, like me, was forced to survive on common sense. He concluded that I could fill several capacities and would be an asset to the household."

"Not bad, not bad at all," Jared said. He was immensely impressed by William's confidence and ingenuity.

"It's not all roses you know," William continued. They had finished their repast and had begun walking back to the *Canton*. "The doctor pays next to nothing. He's a crotchety old man, I must say. My goal is to get back up north to my uncle."

Just then William noticed a highboy dangling precariously from two ragged lines above the cargo hold of the ship.

"I'd best be off this instant," William said. He took off at such a frantic pace that it seemed to Jared as though he planned single-handedly to rescue Mr. Franklin's piece of furniture. "Careful! Careful!" he shouted to the mariners who were handling his goods.

I'd best be off as well, Jared thought. He had almost forgotten why he had come to the docks in the first place. On his list he noted the street number for Mr. William Wills's Pewter Shop and proceeded to the shop's side alley entrance. The counter was full of tankards, candlesticks, and small dishes suitable, Jared noticed, for ashes.

"How do you do," he said aggressively to the craftsman. "How much for the lot?"

"Everything?" Mr. Wills asked incredulously. "You want to clean me out?"

"That's what I said," Jared answered.

"Give me a minute to figure it up," the flustered craftsman said, scratching his head and wondering if Jared planned to take the goods with him.

"I would appreciate it if you could deliver them to the State House straightaway. They're to be used by the delegates to the Constitutional Convention."

"Oh, I see," Mr. Wills said, his eyes lighting up at the thought of the tidy profit he stood a chance to make. He refigured and looked up. "How does twelve pounds sound to you?"

Jared tried to estimate whether he was getting a fair price. He quickly added up the larger objects and concluded that he was not being taken too badly. *Perhaps,* he thought, *I might try bargaining with Mr. Wills to lower the price another two pounds. But why shouldn't the man make a bit of a profit? After all,* Jared reasoned, *his pewterware is the best the city has to offer.* "The price sounds fine with me, Mr. Wills," Jared said, extending his hand to shake on the transaction.

"Young man, I'll need a guarantee of payment before I can deliver your order. I hear tell the Continental Congress is having a hard time meeting its debts, and I can't imagine this Convention being any better off," he said, looking over the top of his metal glasses.

"Don't you worry, Mr. Wills," Jared said with shaky confidence, "some of our city's merchants are underwriting these expenses. You'll get your money in short order."

The work he was sent to do in the next few days was similar. Although the errands looked fairly simple on paper, Jared found them arduous and time-consuming.

One day he spent several hours doing nothing more than narrowing down the list of printers, and another day he devoted a good deal of his time to making preparations for the purchase of stationery items. After his dealings with William Wills, Jared decided he could make a better deal at Robert Aiken's Stationer than he could at the prestigious Dunlap and Claypoole.

Robert Aiken's shop was bright and airy and was designed that way, Jared supposed, so that the workers could set type and inspect the fine print. As he walked in, Jared saw Mr. Aiken seated on a high stool behind the mass of presses, editing a series of advertisements for the *Independent Gazette.* Several apprentices worked steadily, gluing the binding together on an enormous stack of ledgers. Subtle in color, yet elegant and sturdy-looking, their deep brown leather covers seemed most appropriate for delegate use. As Jared gazed about the shelves looking for quills and ink, several distinguished gentlemen, engrossed in political discussion, entered.

"Really now," a portly Southern man said, "why would Washington bother meeting with an Indian?"

Jared moved to a less conspicuous spot, hoping to acquire information for Mr. Madison. He had found that on many of his errands, if he kept his ears open, he could pick up all manner of relevant information.

"Well, I understand he's a Cherokee emissary," another man volunteered. "You really should be grateful that we have a general who seems interested in taking all the citizens into consideration. Perhaps a simple meeting with Sconstayal is all that is needed to quell the Indians' fears."

"Sconstayal, you say!" a third, younger man chimed in. "We, from the Carolinas, take very seriously what he has to say, and you should, too," he asserted, pointing his finger at the portly man. "There is great fear amongst the Indians that we will take their land away, and I must admit their fears are well-founded. Our tobacco fields get bigger each year."

"It's your generation that the Constitution will benefit, Mr. Butler. I should think you'd care more about your property and less about the savages."

Noticing that other patrons were listening to their conversation, the mediator among them suggested that perhaps General Washington was meeting with many such people so that their issues would not infringe on the delegates' time when they began the actual writing of the Constitution. The speaker then put off further discussion by turning to the counter and asking the clerk if he might see a portable writing table.

Jared completed placing his order with Mr. Aiken. After carefully noting the prices of all items, he informed the printer that he would pick everything up and bring the appropriate sum of money on the morrow.

With the feeling of a major task behind him, Jared headed for the City Tavern, where he would check the delegate count. The

City Tavern was another veritable hotbed of conversation and deal-making. Patrons gathered in the Subscription Room to converse. Jared found that if he positioned himself nearby, he could pick up all sorts of information for Mr. Madison.

But today, Friday, he would forgo the eavesdropping because he had a date! Finally, Hetty had given him the signal from her parlor window. They were to meet in the Yard at three o'clock.

He quickened his pace, wanting to have time to relax and get himself together. Once inside, he ordered a drink, found a corner bench, and leaned his back against the wall. It had been almost a week since he had seen Hetty. His stomach knotted with anticipation, as he found himself hoping that everything would go as well as it had on Sunday.

CHAPTER FIVE

BEFORE Jared knew it, the tavern clock struck half after two. He rose quickly and made his way out the door, stopping at a pump to clean up. The cool water felt good against his flushed cheeks. After washing his face Jared used his still-damp hands to smooth back his thick, disheveled hair, tightening the leather rope that held it in place at the nape of his neck.

That done, he took a deep breath and headed for the State House Yard. Jared entered from the west side and stood atop a knoll gazing about the three-block park for Hetty. She was sitting under a delicate willow tree, her bright yellow skirt spread out, forming a circle against the grass. Intent upon her sketching, she didn't notice Jared until he came up beside her.

"Jared, it's you," she said softly, her concentration still on the figures she was drawing.

"We did agree to meet at three, didn't we?" he asked, worried that he had arrived too early.

"Oh yes, silly." She put her pencils back in their case and gave Jared her undivided attention. "I just wanted to finish this outline. What do you think?" she asked, holding her drawing board out for him to see.

"My, my," Jared said enthusiastically. "You really do have a flair, Hetty. I can't even draw stick figures!"

She laughed. "But there are so many other things you can do that I can't."

Jared sat down on the grass near her. Pulling his knees into his body and wrapping his arms around them, he realized how good it felt to relax.

"Tell me what you've been doing; your job sounds so exciting," Hetty said with a smile.

"Well, bargaining with merchants and taking a daily delegate count has been somewhat tedious. But what I'm really enjoying is the fascinating people I'm coming in contact with."

"Such as?" she asked.

"Aside from some of the more pompous delegates, I've had occasion to get to know some of the help."

"The help?" Hetty said, sounding puzzled.

"Hetty, you know that because of our social station both our families limit the company we keep to those people and friends with similar backgrounds."

"That's true, of course," she answered, a small sigh noticeable in her voice.

"Well, I'm beginning to really enjoy spending time with an English chap—William Ellsworth's his name—he's houseboy to Ben Franklin. I'll tell you one thing, he has lived five lives already."

"Really!" she exclaimed. Her brown eyes sparkled at Jared's enthusiasm.

"I could spend hours telling you about William, but you'll meet him soon. Then there's Henry, who works at the Indian Queen. He's from Georgia. He's a slave, belongs to Abraham Baldwin, but the surprising thing is that he's educated!"

"A slave!" she exclaimed. "Oh, Jared, I wish I were allowed to do the things you're doing," she said longingly. "My summer hasn't been one-half as exciting. I come here upon Mr. Peale's instructions, take my regular drawing classes twice a week, and when I'm not

*The State House Yard, with a southwest view
of Walnut Street and the prison*

sketching, or stitching, or listening to my friends talk nonsense, I'm helping Mother pour tea at her numerous afternoon social gatherings. Tell me more!" she said eagerly.

"I suppose the biggest surprise so far has been Mr. Madison's personality. For an exacting man with an austere demeanor, I must admit he is quite interesting and cordial, even supportive of me. Considering the pressure he's under, he really is an amazing man. His patience is being strained every day that the Convention is delayed. But why am I running on about Madison," he caught himself, "when you've met him? Haven't you had him to dinner?"

Hetty nodded.

"Well, what was your impression?"

She pushed her body back so that she could lean against the tree. "If I had to characterize him in one word, I'd say that he is dedicated. He seems to care so very much about what happens to this country."

"You should see how hard he works, Hetty. He makes me feel a bit guilty about taking time off to sit here."

"Oh, I wouldn't want you to feel guilty because of me," she said.

By the tone of her voice, Jared couldn't figure out whether his comment had offended her or whether she was really concerned.

"You needn't stay if you feel uncomfortable," she said.

"No, no, I want to be here, Hetty. Besides, I enjoy exchanging ideas with you. Your insights concerning Mr. Madison will be beneficial to me as I continue to work for him. Surely your father will tell you something of their meetings. I shall be eager to hear of his observations as well."

"My school friends never discuss such things. I love talking with Father about his work and listening to his views about the country, even if Mother *does* say that ladies should be seen and not heard."

Jared felt a smile attempting to shatter his casual expression. *She's so open,* he thought. *She says whatever's on her mind.*

"Oh, I forgot to tell you," Hetty continued, "Mr. Madison noticed my drawings and suggested that I spend some time at the

State House so that I might sketch the delegates as they come and go. Isn't that wonderful?"

"That means you'll be around a good deal this summer."

"I suppose so," she answered coyly, as she began to pack up her things.

The State House clock chimed four times. Jared jumped up. "I must go, Hetty. Shall I stop by again in the morning?" he asked, almost afraid to wait for her answer.

"Please do," she said softly.

Jared sped across the yard, forgoing footways and promenades in deference to time. He was breathless as he barged into the East Room, stopping short at the sight of Dr. Franklin. Jared then realized that he had rushed past the sedan chair outside the building. Had his mind not been on other things, he would have been alerted to Dr. Franklin's presence.

"I beg your pardon," Jared apologized. "I was unaware of your appointment, sir."

"That is quite all right, Jared. Come, sit down." Mr. Madison motioned. "The good doctor and I were only discussing a way in which we might quell the impatience of those representatives already in town. Why don't you tell us who has newly arrived."

Pulling the tattered list from his waistcoat pocket, Jared said, "You'll be pleased with today's news, sir. Several more have arrived. Mrs. House greeted the Honorable Hugh Williamson of North Carolina, and just as I was leaving her place Mr. Gorham's carriage pulled up."

James Madison's eyes met Dr. Franklin's, signaling their approval and seemingly putting to rest Mr. Madison's fear that there would be no Convention at all due to insufficient attendance.

Jared continued. "Rufus King checked into the Indian Queen a few days ago. He was exhausted and mud-splattered, having traveled through a dreadful New England storm. Perhaps that explains the delay of the others from those colonies. And I think I told you already, sir, that Abraham Baldwin is in chamber nine at the Indian

Queen and Jona Dayton is boarding there as well. He made quite an entrance and gave their livery boy a severe dressing down."

Jared wished he could ask both men's opinions of Dayton. Could they be as impressed with him as Uncle Thomas was?

"Any news of Alexander Hamilton?" Mr. Madison inquired.

"No, sir."

"I hope he arrives soon. There is not a stronger Federalist in the country, am I not right, Doctor?"

"That's true, James, but he comes with much baggage. I hear that New York intends to send Yates and Lansing as well. Neither man is too keen on a strong federal government. The powers that be in New York are against not only us, but Hamilton as well. He has his biggest challenge ahead of him."

"Then tomorrow," Jared continued, adding some good news to offset the bad, "the *Charleston* is due in. She's the passenger ship that runs between here and the Carolinas, Mr. Madison. According to the Coastwise Packet Company's clerk, John Rutledge and several other Carolinians are expected to be aboard."

"Very thorough findings, very thorough indeed."

Jared was pleased with Mr. Madison's compliment. "There's more, Mr. Madison," he said excitedly, remembering that he had recorded further notes on a tablet. "Governor Randolph and Dr. McClurg are due in by stage this evening . . . that is, if the ferry is running on time. Shouldn't that complete the Virginia delegation?"

The two men nodded.

"They are to be staying at Mrs. House's as well. Of course, you know that all the important Pennsylvanians are ready and waiting." They all chuckled at Jared's humor; Pennsylvania had been ready for months.

"Well, according to my informal count, we have representatives from six of the colonies. We need representation from one more to have a majority, is that not correct, Dr. Franklin?" Mr. Madison asked.

"Indeed," he answered thoughtfully and paused a moment before continuing. "I couldn't help but imagine, as Jared was reading off the names, what hardship these men have endured en route. They should be rewarded for their efforts . . . perhaps I will arrange a banquet. Yes, indeed," he said, leaning back in his chair, his broad face lighting up at the thought of such a grand idea, "a formal dinner party is befitting such an occasion. What do you think, James? Do you not believe that good feelings flow frequently with the gastric juices?"

"I couldn't agree with you more, Doctor," James Madison answered, his own face showing enthusiasm at the idea of an evening's entertainment and a break from his normal work routine.

Despite the contagious mood, Jared tried to stifle his smile. Everyone in town knew of the joy Dr. Franklin found in socializing.

"Then it's settled," Dr. Franklin said, pounding the floor with his silver-tipped cane. "I've a rare cask of port that is begging to be opened—been saving it for just such an occasion. So then, shall we say tomorrow evening, about half after five?"

"Perfect," Mr. Madison replied. "Would you like Jared to extend your invitations, sir, being that he knows who has arrived and where they are boarding?"

"Would you, my boy?" Dr. Franklin asked. "Although my manservant is used to these impromptu gatherings, any extra help will soften the blow."

Jared nodded as Dr. Franklin rose slowly, using his cane for leverage. "You know, James, even though I am eighty-one years of age, I must confess that my greatest pleasure comes with company, a good laugh, a glass, and a song. How many do you suppose we'll have?"

"Twenty-two, excluding those of us in this room," Mr. Madison replied, precise as usual.

"Twenty-two, aye?" he said, shaking his head. "I'll have to see what I can do about hiring extra kitchen help."

Jared's mind raced, and he immediately thought of Henry Blair. Ever since he'd met Henry he'd felt a desire to do something for the hard-working young man. Knowing that Henry was anxious to earn an extra shilling or two, he mentioned his name.

"Fine, fine," Dr. Franklin answered, pleased not to be burdened with such arrangements. "Have him report to William Ellsworth around five." Dr. Franklin hobbled toward the doorway, his gait a bit more sprightly than usual. "Now that everything's settled, I'll be going. Nice talking with you, James." Taking his leave, all that could be heard was the sound of a cane tapping its way down the empty corridor.

"Well, sir, I'll be off to the Indian Queen," Jared said, "if you are no longer in need of my services."

"I'll be leaving as well," Mr. Madison said. "See you tomorrow."

"Psst, Henry, are you alone?" Jared needed to ask because it had become apparent from his daily visits that livery servants were not expected to socialize while on duty.

"Wait a bit," Henry whispered from inside the Indian Queen's stable, "I got to fetch another bucket of feed, and then I'm done for the night."

Jared waited behind a slick black carriage. Henry appeared minutes later.

"Did you work on this carriage?"

Henry nodded.

"You certainly do a thorough job. These brass lanterns glow. I can even see my reflection on the door!"

Henry beamed. Compliments rarely came his way. "Well, Mastuh Jared, good way to pass time when I'm not tendin' to the animals. I got me some extra pay, too," Henry added, patting the back pocket of his breeches.

"Well, I found another job for you, if you want it and if you can get the time," Jared told him. "Have you ever heard of Benjamin Franklin?"

Henry hadn't.

"No matter," Jared assured him. "He's giving a fancy party

tomorrow night and needs another kitchen boy. I suggested you, thinking you might want to get away from here for once. Besides, I hear tell that when Dr. Franklin has a belly full of drink he's apt to overpay! What do you think?"

"If Mistuh Thompson says he don't need me, I sure will," Henry said eagerly.

"Look, I'll tell Dr. Franklin's houseboy to expect you. You'll like him. He's our age and won't be bothered if you're late in arriving. The banquet is set for half after five, but between Dr. Franklin's inventions, which are always on view, and this heat, the guests will probably linger in the garden as long as possible, and dinner will no doubt be late."

Henry looked pleased. He had been trying for a kitchen job at the Indian Queen, but had gotten no further than washing tankards outside the barroom door. Most nights he did nothing but try to fall asleep amidst the prickly hay, the flies, and the city noise.

"Consider it done then," Jared said. "I've got an idea: would you like to come with me while I deliver the rest of the invitations?"

"You mean go out at night?" Henry asked. "I ain't done nothin' like that before."

"No time like the present, is there?" Jared said. "Wait here while I go inside and ask Mr. Thompson to post a notice about the Franklin party."

There weren't as many stops to make as Jared had thought. Uncle Thomas would be informing the Pennsylvania delegation, James Madison would take care of all the Virginians staying at Mrs. House's. The Indian Queen had the most convention boarders. That left only the City Tavern, the London Coffee House, and a few private homes to visit.

"We'll head for the London Coffee House first," Jared said, attempting to start a conversation. He really hadn't thought much before asking Henry to come with him. It was so unlike Jared to depart from his regular routine and do things like picking up stray friends, especially one who was a slave. And yet, since he had begun his new job, almost everything he did was a departure from the past.

"How do you find city living, Henry?" he asked as they maneuvered around pedestrians out for an evening stroll. People were sitting everywhere, on benches, under awnings, in their kitchen gardens, all trying to escape the heat.

"I ain't seen so many folks in one place ever before," Henry said. "This place never does go to sleep. Back home it's quiet in the daytime and at night. I only see crowds when I drive Mistuh Baldwin into Augusta."

"I used to live in the country, too," Jared said. "But that was a long time ago. My father had a farm out in Bucks County. I don't remember much, but now that you mention it, life was slow, and awfully quiet, too."

They turned right onto Second Street and cut through Taylor's Alley.

"There it is, Henry—the London Coffee House," Jared announced. "It's one of the fanciest spots in town. Want to come inside?"

"Nosuh," Henry answered. "It's best if I just sit right here on this bench till you finish your business." Jared watched him for a moment; Henry was doing his best to absorb the activity all at once.

He had a fairly good idea what Henry was thinking, because he, too, had felt it when he first came to the city. The streets in Philadelphia had their own distinct flavor—almost as though each one represented a separate township. It was one of the things that had fascinated Jared most about the city.

"Folks dress dependin' on who they are and what they do," Henry said, almost to himself. "In every part of town I been to, I find myself tryin' to figure who is who—it's like a game."

The waterfront was cluttered with sailors from the world over. And here on the street that housed the London Coffee House, merchants, sea captains, sailors, and wenches roamed about, all working hard, it seemed, to combine business with pleasure.

A beautiful girl emerged from the side alley carrying a basket full of fruit. She had skin the color of Henry's and lovely almond-shaped eyes that were, at that moment, meeting his. She slowed almost to a full stop, smiled at him, then ran up the steps and into the front door of a building across the street. Henry decided he'd had enough of sitting on the bench and crossed the street to follow her. As he was about to climb the stairs she had taken, he was without warning forced to back up in order to make room for the three men who exploded out of the tavern.

"See you tomorrow," one of them said to the others. "The slave auction commences at nine sharp—got some good strong bodies, I hear."

"And then we'll stay around for the eleven o'clock horse trade," another shouted.

" 'Til tomorrow." They tipped their hats and disappeared.

Henry froze. A slave auction . . . in Philadelphia. . . . Instead of proceeding inside, he simply sat down on the bottom step. He stared blankly, seeing nothing but the brick pattern of the footways beneath his feet.

"Henry," Jared called, when he emerged from the alleyway and did not find his friend where he left him. "Oh, there you are. Well, that's one place down. C'mon," he motioned, "our next stop is the City Tavern."

He started up the footway at a brisk clip, unaware that Henry had not moved from his place on the step. Slowly, Henry got to his feet and started walking after Jared.

"What's wrong?" Jared asked when he slowed enough that Henry finally caught up to him.

"Nothin', suh, I s'pose," he said reluctantly. "I just can't believe what I heard back there."

"What's that?" Jared asked, not taking Henry's angst seriously.

"Slave auctions," Henry said, "right here in Philadelphia! I sure didn't think there'd be that up here."

"Henry, what are you talking about? You aren't making any sense at all."

"Some men comin' out of that coffee house say there's a slave auction t'morrow mornin' right back there where we was, and I'm goin' to go and see for myself," he asserted, his voice getting angrier by the word. "My momma and poppa got bought at an auction, y'know. Them white men make you stand on a big stone block and take off your clothes while other people stare and barter for you. It's one reason I came away from home. To see if thin's are different here."

"It *is* different, Henry," Jared tried to sound convincing. He certainly had never witnessed an auction at the Coffee House. "Your people are treated with respect here, Henry. See over there," he pointed to a simple red brick building. "That's the Negro Schoolhouse started by a friend of my uncle's—a Mr. Benezet. Although most black folk are servants, that's quite a bit different from being a slave. Some get salaries, and the children get schooling if they want it."

"You got any slaves?" Henry challenged Jared.

Wishing he didn't have to admit it, Jared struggled for a decent explanation. "Yes, we do. That is, we have Negro men caring for our country home. But," he hastened to add, "they have their own house on the property and even a garden. Besides, there was a law passed in Pennsylvania that any child born to a man presently of slave status will be a free person in twenty years time."

"Twenty years!" Henry exclaimed. "Why, that's half a lifetime."

Jared chuckled. "No, it isn't. The man I work for, James Madison, is thirty-five, and he's young. Anyway, we don't like slavery here in Pennsylvania, Henry. You've got to believe that."

They walked in silence for a while. Jared recalled an advertisement he had seen in the *Gazette* a few months back. It read something like: BILLL OF SALE: TWO NEGRO WOMEN AND THEIR CHILDREN CERTIFIED TO BE GOOD HOUSE WENCHES, HAVING SERVED FIVE YEARS IN RESPECTABLE HOUSEHOLDS IN BUCKS COUNTY. 200 POUNDS APIECE. Maybe Henry had heard right; Jared knew that Uncle Thomas would never expose him to such a thing. Maybe auctions did take place and he was simply unaware.

After stopping at the City Tavern they headed home, cutting through Trotter's Lane. The deadly silence between the two was broken by the shouts of young voices coming from the next street.

"By golly, Henry! I believe those are my school chums having a game of skittle ball. Let's go see!" Jared ran off ahead and was not surprised to find Jonathan along with Ebin Lewis and the rest of the crowd bowling in the alleyway.

"Jared!" Jonathan said, just as he was about to take his shot. "What brings you here? I told everyone we wouldn't be seeing much of our old friend this summer."

The game stopped and everyone came over to greet Jared. It felt good to be with his school friends, and he suddenly realized how drastically the Convention had altered his plans for the summer. He hadn't seen everyone together since commencement.

"Want to join in? We just got started," Ebin asked.

"We're planning to visit the City Tavern for some ale and a game of whist afterward," Jonathan interrupted.

Jared thought for a minute. Whist was his favorite card game. "Afraid not . . . I'm on duty again."

Henry had been watching from the far end of the alley. He was huddled up against the wall, the ivy providing him with a camouflage.

"I got to get back, Mastuh Jared," he called out finally. His voice quivered, but Henry struggled to control his uneasiness and disguise his discomfort.

"Henry, wait a minute," Jared responded, realizing he had forgotten about him. Henry darted across the alley and out of sight as Jared ran to rejoin him. "Henry! Come back!" Jared called out in vain.

"Who was that?" Ebin asked. "Don't tell me you've taken to fraternizing with servants, and black ones, too!"

"I see you're still cocky," Jared said, his cheeks burning from anger he didn't know he possessed.

"C'mon, Jared, don't be so serious. This job of yours is having its effects," Jonathan piped up, attempting to quell the rage and perhaps divert a fight.

"It's my job to be serious," Jared asserted. "And since I shan't be such good company, I'll pass on your invitation to cards."

He turned and walked proudly down the alley. However, once around the corner Jared put his hands in his pockets and his head down. He was confused, very confused. *Should I go after Henry?* Jared wondered. *No, probably best leave him alone. Nothing I say now will help him feel any better.* Just one week ago, he was one of them. Now he didn't know who he was. One thing was certain, his exposure to Hetty, James Madison, and Henry had changed him.

CHAPTER SIX

JARED had to endure another week of errands before the Convention officially got under way. He hurried through the rainy morning in order to greet Mr. Madison's arrival at the State House.

"Well, Jared m'boy, for once you beat me here. I hope this rain doesn't dampen everyone's spirits," Mr. Madison said, skipping up the steps two at a time.

"After you," Jared gestured grandly, bowing as he pulled open the door.

"Such treatment befits only kings," Mr. Madison chuckled, clearly pleased not only with Jared's treatment but also the fact that opening day had finally arrived. "Surely we should have no thoughts of monarchies today."

"No, sir," Jared countered as they proceeded down the corridor, "but you do deserve some special treatment. You may not be a king, but this group meeting here today has come largely because of your efforts. Am I not right, sir?"

"I played my part, Jared, that much is true. But the important thing to remember is that a historic moment is at hand, regardless of who organized it." Once inside the East Room, Jared double-checked that every conceivable item at the delegates' tables was in its proper place.

"I chose this seat," Mr. Madison said, pointing to a chair directly in front of the presiding member. "What do you think? I shall be seated with members on both my right and my left and will be in a most favorable position for hearing all that is read from the chair and spoken by the members."

"I think your choice has merit, sir. One thing is certain: You, of all those in attendance, will keep the most careful of records."

"That was precisely my thinking," Mr. Madison answered. Jared watched the statesman as he placed his opening remarks in position, took out his penknife, and sharpened a few extra quills. James Madison was biding his time until the first delegate appeared at the door.

"Is there any way I may be of help, sir?" Mr. Fry asked from the doorway, where he stood buttoning his waistcoat.

Judging by Mr. Madison's reaction to the interruption, Jared was sure that he, too, had discovered that Fry was not one to depend on. "I shan't think so, Mr. Fry, at least not at the moment. I do want you to be aware that Master Mifflin is to be considered a personal aide and as such will officially greet each delegate this morning. Further, he is to have access to me whenever he chooses and for that matter, he has free run of the entire State House. Do you understand?"

"Indeed, sir," Mr. Fry agreed, humbled by Mr. Madison's demeanor. The glance Mr. Fry gave Jared as he left was anything but cordial.

As the clock chimed nine times, Jared hurried to his post. The first of twenty-nine delegates was just arriving. He tried to pick out those who he knew had taken part in the Revolution, and found he was more fascinated with the war heroes than the others. Many had been a part of Uncle Thomas's stories—now they were coming to life.

Jared stood almost at attention. "Good day to you, Mr. Butler."

Pierce Butler smiled and nodded in return. Jared had heard his uncle tell many a story about this dignified South Carolinian. *Unbelievable*, thought Jared, *that an ex-British army officer should be at this Convention.*

The rain was letting up as a large group of delegates entered, leaving their oilcloth capes by the front door. The Pennsylvania delegation arrived en masse, Uncle Thomas leading the way. Focusing on Hetty's father, Jared made sure to catch his attention. Jared hoped Mr. Morris would be impressed by his presence. Uncle Thomas winked, making Jared wonder if his uncle had caught on to his friendship with Hetty.

George Washington entered next, leading his formidable group of Virginians. He walked with stately grace through the corridor. The large brass buttons sparkled on his richly tailored blue jacket. The epaulets tacked to his shoulders set him apart from the others. So did his demeanor. To Jared he seemed older than the rest and tired, as though the war had drained him of his energy. He had given so much to achieve independence—it seemed that now he was destined to finish the job.

He and Virginia's Governor Randolph were murmuring last-minute details, Jared supposed, as they neared the door, the others following behind. By now the din coming from the East Room was most jovial, and Jared felt his enthusiasm rising. Uncle Thomas was right: Jared would be witnessing an important event in America's history. Checking his list, he noted that North Carolina's William Davis was still missing. And where was Hamilton? Alexander Hamilton was the man Jared most wanted to meet. He had been one of the generals at the Battle of Princeton. He had so many unanswered questions about that battle. It was the one war story for which Uncle Thomas seemed to have no details. Perhaps General Hamilton had even known his father!

Jared noted that one other important delegate was absent—Ben Franklin. They couldn't start without him.

However, he didn't have to wait long for an answer; the front door opened a moment later and William Ellsworth came tearing down the hall, more animated than Jared had ever seen him.

"Has it started yet?" he asked, out of breath. "I've a message from the doctor."

"The gavel has yet to sound. Give it here, and I shall take it to Mr. Madison."

William collapsed on the bench, relieved that the door was still open, while Jared carried the note in to James Madison. After glancing at the message, Mr. Madison banged the gavel.

"Gentlemen, I call for your attention."

It took several moments for the noise in the room to be silenced because the delegates were standing about in groups, greeting each other and exchanging last-minute notes.

"Dr. Franklin sends his regrets, due to the inclement weather and his feeling out of sorts. He sends not only his good wishes but a message to be read as well, once we are in session. Therefore, gentlemen, with most accounted for, shall we begin?"

Jared took his cue and left the room. He found William waiting for him outside the door. "What a shame about Dr. Franklin," Jared said. "I do hope it's not serious. Mr. Madison says that without him this Convention has not a prayer of reaching resolution."

"Just a touch of rheumatism," William answered. "He says that he always stiffens up from the dampness."

"Some day, isn't it?" Jared asked enthusiastically. His comment was greeted by a blank stare. "I mean for the country," he explained.

"If you say so," William answered. "As far as I can see, you've got yourself a bunch of pompous old men in there."

"How would you know?" Jared asked indignantly.

"I got an eyeful at old Franklin's dinner."

"Dr. Franklin's dinners are not any different than those given by others of his station, I'm sure," Jared said in an attempt to put William in his place.

"When that old man entertains," William began, "everyone knows they're in for a long evening. The doctor literally holds court in his garden until all are present."

"That doesn't sound like Dr. Franklin," Jared said. "He may have become a rich man, but he dresses and acts as he always did.

Do you know he was the talk of Europe, everyone referring to his simple clothing and informal manner?"

"It's just that everyone who comes to the house seems to have a thousand questions for him: What was France like? How are his inventions doing? Where did he find such delicious wine? How is the newspaper business? The bloke has his fingers in everything!"

"So tell me, what happened after the amenities in the garden?"

"Mind you, they finished a cask of port before dinner even commenced. It didn't take long for the jolly attitude of even the most austere gentlemen to express itself."

"Most of them are old acquaintances from the war, you know," Jared informed him.

"They certainly acted like it," William cackled. "Seemed to me they had just won a major battle. Come to think of it, by the time I was ordered to uncork a case of French wine, the conversation was all battles . . . the Battle of Princeton, the Battle of York. They chastised the redcoats something fierce, and with each passing hour the mood became louder and more lively."

"I couldn't believe it when Uncle Thomas stumbled in at dawn, but I'm now beginning to understand," Jared said.

"Are you joking?" William answered. "The meal itself wasn't served until half after nine, for heaven's sake, not because it wasn't ready, but rather because guests wanted to tour the laboratory, or see the inventions. Four or five blokes cornered Washington in the library—to discuss politics, I presume. Finally, Henry and I began serving. Of course, for such an occasion the dear old doctor wouldn't think of serving less than seven courses. Can you imagine how many dishes we had to wash?"

Jared shook his head in amazement.

"And then they began the toasts! The general was at the head of the table. For all the talk about him being quiet and stately, he became the most boisterous of the lot with his toasts. First he raised his glass to the country. Then, of course, to the host. And after that the man insisted on toasting everyone with whom he was dining and finishing a whole glass of wine with each person! It's amazing he could depart the evening on his own accord!"

"I can't believe it," Jared said. "Not General Washington."

"I tell the truth, Jared. But I must say, he continued to remain a model of decorum throughout the evening and certainly had more gentlemanly presence than any of the others."

"Such as?" Jared was terribly curious now, wondering if Uncle Thomas or anyone else he knew had misbehaved.

"Well, William Temple Franklin made a bit of a fool of himself chasing Lucy Fitzsimmons around the parlor while the others contented themselves with cigars and harpsichord music. And finding Mr. Lansing's body draped over the settee the following morning was a bit of a shock. He was so drunk, he couldn't find his way home. Other than those two incidents, I suppose the group was a model of decorum. To be perfectly honest, I'm mostly put off by the stuffiness of the southerners; you know, the ones who look and act as though they are a cut above the rest. And they were boasting about their slaves, in front of Henry, too. They spent a good deal of time comparing how many slaves each man owned, as if the number represented someone's status and wealth."

"Well, in fact, it does," Jared explained. "My uncle is taxed for every servant we have, right along with the rest of our possessions and property."

"People as property!" William bellowed. "I, for one, will never be mere property." He paused a moment to ponder what he had said. Looking at Jared with fear in his eyes, he asked, "Do you suppose Dr. Franklin pays for me? Am I his property?"

"I really don't know," Jared lied.

"I guess I'm only one step above a slave, then?" William said. "If I didn't have an incentive for getting myself back to Massachusetts before, I assuredly do now." He stood up, obviously ready to leave. "I'm glad we had this discussion, Jared," he said with resolve. "I'd best get back to my charge. When the doctor is laid up it gives me extra time, perhaps enough to pick up some extra money. Cheerio, then."

The sound of William's footsteps was muffled by the banging of canes within the chamber. Jared knew that to be a sign of some sort of agreement. Inching his body along the bench, he positioned himself close to the still open door.

"So, gentlemen," Mr. Madison began, "we have among us the collective wisdom of the continent, according to this article in the *New York Daily Advisor*." He held the newspaper in the air for all to see. "Our own Dr. Franklin feels that we are an assembly of notables. Let us prove him right and adhere to his warning that once again we must all hang together or most assuredly we shall hang separately."

"Here, here," the delegates agreed.

Jared had opened the door just a hair more in order to have a better view. "And as a first act Benjamin Franklin entreats us to hesitate not," Mr. Madison read from Franklin's message, "to nominate General George Washington to preside over this grand Convention."

Jared quickly glanced in the general's direction; his face registered not only surprise but a shyness and a humble look as well.

"I might add here," Mr. Madison continued, "that this nomination comes with particular grace as our good doctor could himself be a likely candidate."

"Here, here," the body of men chanted.

Just then Jared heard the voice of Robert Morris as he rose to his feet and formally seconded the motion.

Mr. Morris escorted the general to the speaker's chair. Before allowing himself to sit, the general looked out at the body of friends and colleagues and said: "In what we do here, let us raise a standard to which the wise are honest."

"Here, here," Robert Lansing of New York exclaimed, jumping to his feet. "And may I add, that any act whatsoever of so respectable a body must have a great effect upon this nation, and if we do not succeed great dissension among the colonies will follow."

Just then William returned, having forgotten his pouch. Jared carefully shut the door, announcing that General Washington had just been made president of the Convention. "Other than Mr. Madison, he deserves the honor most," Jared said jauntily.

"Oh, really, a military man as head of a government? I'm not so sure that's a good idea," William said, baiting Jared.

"Wait a minute. You come over here from England to be a free man and then make a mockery of our heroes? I'll have you know my father died for that military man, and I'll not have a common Englishman speak disparagingly of him."

"Look, Jared, I've not time for another discussion. The doctor wants me to bring him news of the proceedings, and if I know him he'll be hammering his cane against the wall, going slightly crazy if I don't get back there right away. No hard feelings, now. We just look at things a bit differently, right?" He patted Jared on the back and left.

As Jared sat, his hands folded in his lap, thoughts ajumble in his mind, he couldn't help but hear a voice—a southerner, he determined—proposing an assortment of rules and guidelines. Not able to restrain himself, he gently turned the doorknob and peered inside, noticing that it was Richard Dobbs Spaight, one of the youngest delegates, who was speaking.

"Members are forbidden to whisper, read, or pass notes while one of their colleagues is speaking; a call to order may be uttered by any member; and when the house shall adjourn, every member shall stand in his place until the president passes him."

Mr. Fry sat on the other side of the door. Jared glanced over at him and mused at what an odd-looking pair they must present to the citizens wandering up and down the halls. Jared wasn't particularly interested in listening to the delegates read their credentials, so he leaned his back against the wall and tried to make sense of his conversation with William.

For all his controversial statements, William's opinions were those of someone who most definitely had a mind of his own. No one had molded William Ellsworth. One thing that bothered Jared about being adopted was that he'd been thrust into an upper-class urban life without having any say in the matter. He also disliked feeling so indebted to Uncle Thomas and Aunt Sarah that he had to be what they wanted and give up something of himself in the process. William's determination to be free was enviable.

Jared was lost in these thoughts and unaware of the passing time, but all at once he heard the gavel sound. As the doors burst open, he quickly jumped to attention, smiling at each representative and noticing that they all seemed more serious departing than when they had arrived.

General Washington had been the first to depart. He cut a lonely figure as he made his way down the corridor. Jared wasted no time getting into the East Room to hear firsthand from James Madison what had transpired. Mr. Madison was slouched in his chair, looking as though he had just run a race and won.

"May I ask how your day went?" Jared questioned. "Perhaps it's none of my business, sir, but I do hope you are feeling satisfied."

"Jared, my boy, I can only tell you that precisely what I had hoped would take place, did. We have a chance, by God," he said, slapping his fist upon the table. "We have a chance to succeed with this Constitution."

"How can you be so sure?"

"Have you heard me speak of Richard Spaight? He's a bright young fellow, a North Carolinian—commanded his own unit during the war, served on the Continental Congress. Well, anyway, unbeknownst to me he took it upon himself to request that this Convention be kept secret until a decision is reached. Can you believe it? That is what I had hoped for all along. I felt sure the proposal would have to come from me, and then it might not have been so readily accepted."

Jared had known this was important to Mr. Madison, but he was bewildered at seeing the man so animated.

"You see, Jared, only in an atmosphere free of publicity and external pressures will men of this caliber speak freely, not only from their minds but from their hearts as well. They don't want to be thought the fool back home, you know. And we need their honest opinions if we are to write a Constitution worthy of this land. There is so much at stake," he continued. "Should we be swayed by public opinion at this point, we're finished. Do you understand?"

"I think so." Jared couldn't help thinking of William's comments and his questions about how democratic the Convention would actually be.

"Your job will take on a new meaning now," Mr. Madison continued. "I could hear stirrings in the hallways throughout the day, as well as crowds gathering by the windows. From this point on, you must keep the citizenry a good distance away and the corridor clear of those that loiter. We must not be overheard."

"I'm beginning to understand, sir," Jared answered. "But what am I to say to the writers from the *Packett* and the *Gazette*? They sat in the hallway the entire day waiting for a crumb of information. I must say, sir, that they were not pleased when the doors finally opened at the end of the session and no delegate did more than smile at them."

"We shall put a notice out to the newspapers in due time. Until then, Jared, handle them as best you can."

CHAPTER SEVEN

H IS work was cut out for him, of that Jared was sure. As he
meandered home, he wondered how he could control the
constant traffic in and around the building, guard the door, and be
available for Mr. Madison all at the same time. Jared passed Hetty's
house and lingered across the street on the chance that she might
pass en route to or from home. He wished it were proper to walk
up, knock on the door, and ask to see her. Right now he needed to
talk—about the day, about the weeks to come, about his feelings.
Although surrounded by people all day, he was at the same time iso-
lated. Jared leaned against one of the trees that lined Market Street for
a few more minutes, then gave up and continued home. If he couldn't
talk to Hetty, the next best thing would be to write a letter to her.

The house was unusually quiet; even Margaret and Annie were
nowhere to be found. Grabbing a couple of muffins and a mug of
lemonade, Jared headed for his room to collect his thoughts.

Friday, 25th May

Dear Hetty,

 *My mind is reeling with thoughts and feelings about the
events of today, so I wanted to share them with you. Waiting
to tell you everything is just impossible.*

"Jared! Jared! Are you up there?" Uncle Thomas called, breaking Jared's train of thought. Jared slammed his ledger shut and answered.

"Well, c'mon, boy. We're waiting dinner for you, and we didn't know where you were! I have a meeting at the Indian Queen in one hour's time." When Jared appeared at the top of the staircase, his uncle continued. "Mr. Madison thinks it would be good for you to come along so that you can familiarize yourself with some of the Virginia delegates."

"I'll be right down," Jared answered. Although he had hoped for a few hours of solitude, he was not displeased that James Madison had requested his presence. *I'll finish Hetty's note tomorrow*, he promised himself, tucking his ledger under his pillow and heading down to the family.

Had Jared realized that that was his last free moment all weekend, he wouldn't have jumped so quickly in response to Uncle Thomas's call.

Saturday seemed bearable only because Jared knew he would be seeing Hetty after church the following day. But that afternoon Uncle Thomas announced that the family would be departing for their country home directly after meeting and that several delegates would be joining them!

And so, by Monday, Jared was bleary-eyed and agitated. He went through the motions of greeting each delegate, but their faces blended together until Jared couldn't tell one from another. He hadn't even had a moment to tell Hetty of his family's plans. He was sure she must be thinking of him as an ill-mannered cad. His days seemed to promise little else but one menial task after another, and when he wasn't serving Mr. Madison, he seemed to be running here and there for Uncle Thomas. And now he was expected to control the spectators. Jared was becoming more and more disillusioned with his job and his summer.

The State House was bustling with activity almost every day because the Supreme Court was in session directly across the hall.

Spectators packed the open room and overflowed into the hall. It was impossible to handle all the people.

If this is how the summer is going to be, he thought, *I am certain to go crazy.*

It wasn't until Thursday that Jared found himself with a spare moment to delve back into his thoughts and finish his letter to Hetty:

> *. . . it's been six days since I began this! Oh, Hetty, I do hope you'll understand. My schedule is crazy. I am literally at everyone's beck and call. What was supposed to be a summer of freedom has turned into a period of restriction. Before I say another thing, and if I haven't blackened my name with you, would you be able to see me after church this Sunday? I'd like to explain about this last Sunday in person. Margaret could prepare a picnic, and we could walk by the river—*

"What are you up to, old boy?" William asked, looking over Jared's right shoulder. "Doing personal business on the job, aye?"

"William! How dare you sneak up on me like that!" Jared said, feeling a bit foolish and slamming his book shut. "Besides, I'm not taking notes . . . just writing a letter to a lady friend."

"A lady?" William chided him further. "Who's the lucky girl, or should I say, what did you ever do to deserve such a pleasure?"

Jared's cheeks flushed. "Ellsworth, you are too nosy for your own good! However, I do admit it's a good distraction—the girl, I mean—as the days tend to run on endlessly. I must say, I envy your mobility. Hetty and I—her name is Hetty Morris—had planned to meet once in a while in the State House Yard when the delegates stopped to caucus, but so far they haven't stopped for anything. I decided that writing letters is my only hope of keeping her interest."

"I've always found the ladies like any sort of attention you pay them."

"You fancy yourself to be quite the rogue, don't you?" Jared asked, curious as to whether William really had experience with girls or was just bluffing his way through another conversation.

They were interrupted by the trial in progress across the way.

"Order in the Court! Order, I say," the judge yelled, pounding his gavel. "Do not insult my ears once more with your Bellingsgate language," he said, chastising the three pitiful-looking men hanging onto the bars of the prisoners' cage situated inside the room.

"Looks like something's about to happen," William said excitedly. "If we stand right up here on your bench we'll get a good view of what's going on. I heard someone say that those three blokes have been accused of robbing a stand at the farmer's market."

Jared hadn't taken too much interest in the court up until now, but William's enthusiasm was catching. They towered above the throngs of peasants from atop the bench, and Jared found himself laughing at the sight of Judge McKlean's wig, which in his fervor had slid sideways. The crowd gradually simmered down. *Thank God,* Jared thought. *Mr. Madison is surely going to register his share of complaints about the noise in the corridor today.*

"So be it," Judge McKlean said. "It is the wish of the court that you all be sentenced to one year of prison and an additional year of labor in the city of Philadelphia. Case dismissed." The sound of the gavel hitting the block sounded like a guillotine dropping onto its victim.

As the crowd booed, Jared watched the prisoners being led away. They didn't look evil enough to deserve such a strong sentence.

"I wonder if this was the sort of courtroom scene my uncle endured," William said. "From what I've been observing at these trials, the poor men accused are at the mercy of the judge's mood. A couple of days ago two blokes were let off scot-free after having been accused of attacking a stagecoach at the city limits. And *they* seemed guilty! Oh, well," William concluded, "I've never witnessed justice in any such formal situations. The rich judges are against the poorer citizens. It was that way in England, and it appears no different here." He jumped off the bench and walked down the hall, not bothering to say good-bye.

Jared watched him make his way through the crowd. A man stopped to talk to him. Jared took a closer look. *That's Nehemiah Weaver, from the Pennsylvania Gazette,* he said to himself. *I wonder what he wants with William.*

The *Gazette* was certainly the most respected newspaper in the city. It regularly included important political news—what was taking place in the State Assembly and also in the other colonies. When Uncle Thomas wanted to know the goings-on in New York or Boston, he could find one story a week in the *Gazette* at the very least.

Mr. Weaver had approached Jared on opening day, trying to get a story. He had interviewed Uncle Thomas, and had been asking questions of the delegates since their arrival. *But what could he want with William?* Jared wondered.

The clock struck half after one. "Time for my rounds," Jared told Mr. Fry. His plan was to circle the building hourly, to spot loiterers and discourage them from hanging around. It was the only way he could think of to keep the Convention happenings relatively secret.

There was no one lurking anywhere, not even Hetty under her favorite tree. Jared returned to his post and attempted once more to finish the letter.

"Still writing," William said, striding up the now-quiet hall. "Is that all you do?"

"Why are you back already?" Jared asked. "You just left!"

William took a leather bag out of his pocket. "Medicine, my friend. Dr. Franklin forgot to take his morning dose. He'll be in agony by tonight if he doesn't keep up with his remedies. Have they recessed yet?"

"Are you kidding?" Jared answered sarcastically. "Don't I wish they would; once those doors are closed they're not likely to open before four. Shall I slip in and tell Dr. Franklin you're here?" Jared asked, already off the bench and beside the door. He hadn't had a legitimate reason to enter the chamber when it was in session and was curious to see what the delegates were doing.

Jared took his time, moving quietly toward Dr. Franklin, who was seated front and center, so as to overhear as much of the proceedings as possible. Unfortunately, given the room's dimensions, it didn't take but a minute to reach the doctor. After whispering into his ear, Dr. Franklin grabbed onto Jared's arm and the two walked out together, but not before Jared caught a glimpse of Uncle Thomas, who looked puzzled by his nephew's entrance.

Once outside, the doctor gobbled down his drops. Then he thanked William for remembering, winked at Jared, and immediately returned to work.

"Well, I'll be on my way again," William announced. "I need to pick up some vegetables at the market; the doctor is entertaining again tonight."

"Before you go," Jared said, "I've got a question." They moved away from the door and out of Mr. Fry's hearing. "What business did that curious Mr. Weaver have with you today? I saw him corner you at the end of the hall."

"Who?" William asked absently.

"The writer—you remember—the man with the flaming red hair and big mustache."

"Oh, him! He's just looking for any sort of information I might have from Dr. Franklin on what's happening at the Convention."

"What did you tell him?" Jared asked.

"I tell him anything I overhear Dr. Franklin discussing at home or with friends. You know, things like bringing the small states around slowly so they'll eventually agree with the larger ones."

"You didn't tell him that!" Jared was aghast.

"Why not? Doesn't everyone have a right to know?"

"Certainly," Jared said, "but only after the entire Constitution is written. The delegates have pledged to keep what transpires inside the East Room a secret."

"Well, how was I supposed to know that?" William asked defensively. "And besides, I'm not even a delegate. What's wrong with giving a little information? People are always asking me what the doctor is up to."

"Mr. Madison told me to keep anything I might hear quiet. I would assume the same applies to you. You wouldn't want to lose your job, would you?"

"For telling a tale or two? Dr. Franklin wouldn't discharge me for that. Jared, you worry too much. You could do well to loosen up a bit. Speaking of serious," he said, trying to change the subject, "tell me about your girl."

"There's not much to tell. Mostly I'm concerned about losing her interest at the very beginning of something that might be good. Here I sit with a freshly written letter and probably not a spare minute to deliver it."

"Your day here is finished at five, isn't it?" William asked.

"It's supposed to be, but Mr. Madison has detained me several evenings this week. I never know what will be asked of me."

"I can deliver your letter," William offered. "The Morris mansion—that is the Robert Morrises, isn't it?—isn't far from the doctor's home."

"Would you? I would be much obliged. I'll finish this by the time you come back to pick up Dr. Franklin. . . . William," Jared said as an afterthought, "would you consider a daily arrangement? I mean, if I paid you for your efforts, do you suppose you could drop off my notes on a daily basis?"

"I don't see why not. But Jared, I couldn't think of being paid for such a thing."

"Look at it this way, William. You're doing me a greatly appreciated service. Besides, you need to earn a little extra money. You haven't found another job, have you?"

"Well, I'm working on being a delivery boy for the bakery by the docks. I'm trying to rearrange my schedule so I can deliver bread at dawn and get back to the doctor's in time to do the breakfast dishes. Speaking of which, I told the baker I'd give him a definite answer today. I'd better be on my way. I'll see you later to pick up the letter."

The rest of the day sped by. When the East Room doors opened at half after four, Jared headed in immediately, anxious to get his duties finished. He thought about stopping in to see Jonathan to find out what everyone was up to that night.

Jared was in time to hear Uncle Thomas talking to Mr. Madison. "Tell me, James, how's my nephew doing?"

Embarrassed at overhearing the conversation, Jared busied himself emptying tankards and ashtrays.

"I couldn't manage without him," Mr. Madison answered. "He is more than capable, in fact, he's a valuable asset to me. I think there's a promising future in store for him, if he wants it," Mr. Madison said, gesturing toward Jared.

Uncle Thomas beamed, proud to take some of the credit for Jared's accomplishments.

"Will you require my nephew's services further tonight, James? I'd like him to accompany me home. We've barely spoken since these meetings commenced. It certainly has been a hectic week— but profitable, aye? So far we are moving along at a speed I could never have guessed possible."

"Indeed. Indeed," Mr. Madison replied, now relaxing in his chair with his feet propped up on his table. "Take the young man home with you, Thomas. He could do with a night off. I'm afraid I've detained him later and later each day."

"Very well, then," Uncle Thomas said. After Jared scurried to replace the cleaned ashtrays, they left the State House without delay.

It felt good to be getting away early, but Jared felt a bit like he was being passed from one chain of command to another. And once home, he thought, Aunt Sarah would probably have an enormous family dinner arranged, perhaps even guests present. Suddenly the promise of a free evening did not look so bright.

Managing a cheery front, Jared talked to his uncle about the day's politics. "Aside from the mundane chores," he said, "I have to admit I am learning quite a bit from the delegates as they arrive and depart. And Uncle, I must also admit to a bit of eavesdropping."

"You can't help overhearing some issues," Uncle Thomas said, smiling and winking as was his custom when the two of them shared a private thought. "You simply must show discretion in not divulging the information—our secrecy pact is of vital importance."

"So I'm finding out. In fact, my most important job is to keep the writers at a good distance and suspicious onlookers far from open windows."

Catching up actually felt good, Jared thought. The footways were surprisingly empty. The city seemed calmer than usual, and the humidity had dissipated. Perhaps these were good omens for the weekend to come.

"Well, my boy, we've only two more days of work this week and then Sunday off. I hope you have made some plans for yourself. We can't have one of Philadelphia's fair young men becoming a workhorse."

Jared smiled. "Don't worry, Uncle. I have plans for Sunday."

"That reminds me, your Aunt Sarah and I have invited Robert Morris and his family to dine with us on Sunday. We haven't seen them socially since the winter season. I do hope you'll be available to join us."

Jared could hardly hide his excitement. "That's fine, just fine," he said. "My plans are for earlier in the day."

The walk home passed quickly. Aunt Sarah and the girls welcomed them enthusiastically, pleased to have company after a day alone. Jared excused himself and went to change into comfortable clothes.

Sunday, he thought, grinning as he threw off his jacket and loosened his collar. *I can't wait!*

CHAPTER EIGHT

THE aroma from Margaret's cooking was winding its way up to Jared's room as he dressed for dinner.

The dining room table had been extended to seat ten. Margaret had arranged a centerpiece of fruit into a multicolored pyramid. The house bustled as the hour of arrival approached.

"Can I be of any help, Aunt Sarah?" Jared asked, bounding down the stairs in uncharacteristic enthusiasm. Elizabeth and Mary were running to and from the pantry carrying dishes and silver.

"Would you take the punch bowl and decanter out to the garden?" Aunt Sarah called. "I thought we'd serve the Madeira and lemonade there, and stay outside until the house is cool enough to endure. Once the sun disappears over the rooftops we can retire to the dining room."

Jared whistled as he headed for the pantry to load up a tray. "And dear," Aunt Sarah called after him, "do make sure we have plenty of chairs outside—at least enough for the adults and older children—will you? Do you suppose we should get out a few games for the younger ones?"

"Good idea," Jared called back to her. *If the little ones are occupied and the adults become engrossed in conversation,* he thought, *it will give Hetty and me time to be alone.* He still couldn't believe his good fortune—the Morrises were actually coming to spend the evening!

They arrived precisely at six. The suddenly crowded entrance hall was bursting with energy: friends greeting each other, hats and shawls being removed . . . but Jared saw only one person. Hetty looked radiant in a scarlet dress; a dainty pink velvet ribbon hung around her neck, with a heart-shaped broach attached to it.

"Won't you join us in the garden for a beverage?" Aunt Sarah said, easing the guests through the main hallway and out onto the cozy Mifflin patio.

Jared noticed that Hetty was carrying her portfolio. "Are those some of your sketches?" he asked quietly. She nodded and smiled, having not yet uttered a word. "I'm dying to see what you've been drawing. If we move over to the gazebo, we can lay them out on the wooden floor."

Jared was thrilled that he and Hetty could be alone so soon, but as the two began to drift away from the others, Mr. Morris called out proudly, "Hetty, I'm sure everyone would take pleasure in viewing your sketches."

"If you wish, Father," Hetty answered obligingly and turned back to rejoin the group. She unfastened the string holding her package together and carefully lifted out each rendering, holding it on her lap for everyone to see.

"I have an idea: Why don't you guess who each person is?" Robert Morris suggested. "If my daughter has drawn a decent likeness, one of us should surely be able to attach a name to the picture— at least to the more well-known delegates."

And so the game was on. Jared stood back from the group, a glass of Madeira in his hand, watching Hetty's performance. They guessed Benjamin Franklin, Thomas Fitzsimmons, and, of course, Gouverneur Morris.

"Can you guess this one?" she asked, giggling as they all looked at the portrait of "the governor" with his unmistakable peg leg. "It wasn't hard to get him to sit for me," she teased. Then they all chuckled at the rendering of her father, his round face and jovial

Dr. Benjamin Franklin at the Chestnut Street entrance
of the State House

smile spreading across the paper. "And Mr. Mifflin, I should be honored to draw you next week," Hetty suggested cleverly. She had no intention of letting Jared's uncle feel overlooked.

"You've obviously been busy, my dear," Uncle Thomas answered. "In due time. In due time. I fear it will be a long summer; there will be many an opportunity."

Jared's and Hetty's eyes met, each hoping for a long summer.

Uncle Thomas noticed the eye contact and cleared his throat. Hetty quickly took out another picture. "I must say it is difficult to catch these men coming and going, but here I've drawn some groups of delegates standing in the State House Yard, discussing matters of the day, I presume."

"Ah, yes," Uncle Thomas said. "That group looks like the Virginians. Aha!" He moved closer, pointing to a section of the paper. "And if I'm not mistaken, there are a few New Jersey delegates among them. Very interesting—isn't it, Robert—to see who is chatting with whom." He turned to Hetty. "I don't suppose you can listen to their conversations and sketch at the same time, can you, Hetty?"

"Oh, no, sir," she answered, "but several of the gentlemen have seen me working and have tarried a bit to give me time to complete my outline. If I manage to get a particularly good look at them, I can usually do the portraits from memory later."

Mrs. Morris and Aunt Sarah looked at each other, nodding approval at Hetty's talent.

"Here is one person I did that way—Jona Dayton, I believe. Isn't he from New Jersey?" Hetty asked. Uncle Thomas nodded. "He's awfully handsome, really," Hetty volunteered. "Good bone structure in the face."

"He is quite a young man," Robert Morris said, "the youngest in the group."

"Indeed," Uncle Thomas agreed. "He's forthright, with an excellent reputation from the military. I see big things on the horizon for him."

Jared was becoming ill-humored with all this talk of Dayton. Couldn't they see through the surface and realize that he was an opportunist? Jared noticed that Hetty was smiling at her picture, oblivious to the conversation and Jared's thoughts.

"You know, Hetty, my dear," her father suggested, "you ought to take Mr. Dayton around for a proper sitting with your instructor, Mr. Peale. I know that General Washington has been sitting for a formal portrait, as are some other prominent members. Dayton should surely be included."

Jared was seething now and was about to say something when Hetty answered, "What a good idea, Father. He does seem rather special. I have had occasion to chat with him twice now as he departs the Convention. I shall have to ask him the next time he engages me."

Jared couldn't believe he had heard her say that. He'd have to set her straight and quickly, lest she be further misled by this scoundrel.

"Dinner is served," Margaret announced.

What a blessing, Jared thought. *Anything to put a stop to this conversation.*

Aunt Sarah led the group into the dining room, where seating arrangements were orchestrated. She and Uncle Thomas sat, as was customary, at either end of the table, with Mrs. Morris at her host's right and Mr. Morris at his hostess's. The two Morris brothers, William White and Charles, were instructed to take their places on either side of Elizabeth and Mary. And much to Jared's good fortune, Hetty was seated beside him. Her bouffant skirt brushed against his breeches as he settled into his seat, and he couldn't help but think— while Uncle said the blessing—how nice it felt to have her so near.

Cold salmon was placed in front of everyone. Aunt Sarah hadn't yet taken a bite when she asked, "How are the meetings moving along?" Jared was surprised that she had even brought it up—Aunt Sarah rarely involved herself in her husband's politics. "I don't know about Robert, Mary," Aunt Sarah said to Mrs. Morris, "but Thomas hasn't been home for weeks. I've never seen him care so for anything."

Before Mrs. Morris could answer, Mr. Morris spoke up.

"We're making surprisingly good progress, Sarah, but I fear we are in for a battle during the next few weeks. Am I right, Thomas?" he asked.

"No question about it. The biggest decision lies ahead. If we can reach a compromise, I daresay there is hope of formulating a Constitution."

"And on what issue is it that the members must be agreed, Father?" Hetty piped up.

"Now, dear," Mary Morris cautioned, "this is man's talk."

"I know, Mother, but because Mrs. Mifflin introduced the discussion, I feel I am correct in asking a question now and again. After all, your dear friend Abigail Adams is always telling her husband to remember the ladies. Are we not a part of this country?"

"I couldn't agree with you more," Jared said, defending her spirit and surprising himself. "I, too, feel strongly that what is decided this summer will affect *all* of our generation, perhaps more than any other."

"Well," Uncle Thomas said, again clearing his throat, "Hetty's forthrightness is to be commended. It is rather unexpected coming from a lady, but I find it thoroughly charming. And in answer to your question, the smaller and less populated states fear that they will not be fairly represented in the new Congress. In the next few weeks we must arrive at some decision on representation that is both agreeable and fair to all concerned."

"And aren't there many economic considerations to be taken into account, Uncle?" Jared asked.

"Indeed. My goodness, you have been doing your homework."

"No, actually I've simply been keeping my ears as open as Hetty has been her eyes."

Everyone laughed, and Jared smiled—he had managed to break the tension while making everyone aware that neither he nor Hetty were children any longer. The two of them seemed to have inherited political interests, and both wished to be taken seriously.

"Convention, convention, convention," thirteen-year-old Charles said as Margaret spooned garden vegetables and Annie served the roast duck, "that's all anybody talks about anymore."

"Charles!" his mother said quickly, horrified at his outburst. "If you are to partake of the adult world, dear—and I did hear you beg to be included tonight, did I not—" Mrs. Morris continued, "then we must just sit up straight, keep still, and listen."

"I beg to disagree, Mother," he retorted. "We just determined that it was proper for Hetty to speak." The adults cleared their throats as Hetty and Jared stifled their giggles.

"But dear," Mrs. Morris said, her voice now clearly strained, "Hetty is practically of age, and she is somewhat involved in all this Constitution business."

"I beg your pardon, Mrs. Morris, but I agree with Charles," Elizabeth Mifflin piped up, contributing to the free-for-all. "A family discussion is just that. If we must sit for the duration, you should be proud, Father," she looked fearlessly in his direction and quickly turned to eye her mother, "that any one of us has an opinion!"

"Perhaps we have dwelt on politics a bit too long, Robert," Uncle Thomas said with a half-approving twinkle in his eye. "I must admit to being puffed up a bit at the aggressiveness I see developing in our offspring. Don't you find it refreshing?"

Robert Morris sighed.

Jared found the entire scene humorous. Here sat two of the most outspoken men in Philadelphia—was it any wonder that their children would follow suit?

"I suppose this is just the beginning, Thomas," Robert Morris sighed. "When my other two, Robert and Thomas, return from their studies in England, I daresay they'll have plenty of ideas of their own. Perhaps the days when we're able to monopolize the minds and words of our young are over."

"We are, after all, the next generation, sir," Jared inserted, "and with the country teetering as it is, I'd say it's our obligation to express an interest, regardless of propriety."

"Enough said, then," Aunt Sarah concluded, ringing the dinner bell several seconds longer than usual. Both Annie and Margaret appeared on cue. "I think we're ready for dessert now," she said firmly, clearly hinting that the time had come for lighter conversation.

"You know, Hetty dear," her father said, "I do think that Jared, given the position he's in, should also be the subject of one of your drawings—for posterity's sake."

"What a fine idea, Father," Hetty agreed, looking at Jared as she answered. "When might you be available for a sitting?" she asked coyly.

"I'll have to check my busy schedule," he said, chiding her and making a joke of the entire idea.

Shortly after coffee was served, Aunt Sarah invited the ladies to withdraw to the parlor. Hetty dutifully followed her mother while Jared, wishing he could follow Hetty, joined the men in the study.

"Would you have a cigar, Robert?" Uncle Thomas passed the box around. The Morris boys and Jared settled comfortably onto the horsehair settee while Uncle Thomas and Mr. Morris claimed the two large easy chairs. It was because of these overstuffed, well-worn pieces of furniture that Jared favored this room to any other in the house.

"So, you predict that the battle will begin tomorrow?" Uncle Thomas asked Mr. Morris, who was bending over a candle, attempting to get a good flame going on the tip of his cigar.

"I hear that John Dickenson intends to address the Convention as soon as possible to ask for equal representation in the Senate and a proportionate representation in the House," Mr. Morris answered.

"That should light the fire, all right," Uncle Thomas said. "Are we ready for the fight?"

"Since it was James Madison who informed me of this, I assume he is prepared to mediate the differing factions. With that man at the helm, I'm confident we'll keep on course."

"There will be several new arrivals tomorrow," Jared said. "Perhaps everyone will be on their best behavior for the newcomers."

"You've got a point there, Jared," Uncle Thomas agreed.

Jared's eyes were pulled toward the door where he noticed a flash of scarlet pass by. "Please excuse me," he said, setting down his brandy. He moved quickly into the darkened hallway.

"Hetty," he whispered as he tiptoed down the narrow hall. "Do you suppose we might retreat to the gazebo? I don't know about you, but I've had enough political talk for one night."

"I shouldn't think that any eyebrows would be raised," she answered quickly. "After all, it is awfully stuffy in here, and what harm could there be in two people simply seeking fresh air? Isn't that what a gazebo is for?" she asked. Lifting her skirt slightly, she stepped out the door with saucy assurance.

"I couldn't agree more," Jared said as he followed her.

They walked quickly toward the gazebo, Jared wondering if he should bring up his feelings about Jona Dayton. Hetty chose the smallest bench in the gazebo and sat down, pulling her skirt close to her body and making room for Jared to share the seat.

Once he was comfortable, she readjusted her position, nestling her tiny frame against his side.

"Are you chilly, Hetty?" he asked for want of a better question as she moved even closer. He felt light-headed and carefree, more so than he ever remembered being.

Hetty nodded to indicate that she was as a breeze swept gently through the gazebo.

"Well then, let me keep you warm," he said, lifting his arm and placing it around her shoulder. Jared knew then that he needn't worry about Jona Dayton.

Hetty then startled him further by saying, "I never thought we'd be alone . . . I mean," she caught herself, "I so looked forward to coming to your house for dinner, but mostly I've just been anxious all week, waiting to have a chance to talk to you."

"I feel the same way, Hetty. Isn't it crazy how busy we've been? I never dreamed I would be so involved with the Convention."

"But Jared, it is the chance of a lifetime. You must remember that. We'll have time to do things when it's over."

She turned away—embarrassed, Jared thought, about letting him know she cared so much about seeing him.

Jared reached over and turned her face toward him. Her eyes focused on his, and the world around them drifted away in darkness. It took all the self-control he could muster not to kiss her, right then and there. But he continued to look into her eyes, afraid to blink and break the spell of this quiet moment.

Barely moving, they sat quietly, enjoying the stillness and the melodic chirps of the crickets until a voice from the darkness startled them both.

"Hetty, Hetty dear, are you out there?" It was Mrs. Morris calling. "We must be going home soon."

"Coming, Mother," Hetty answered, jumping up from the bench. Unexpectedly, she planted a kiss on Jared's cheek.

Before Jared could react she was skipping happily toward the house.

With a flush in his cheeks and a lump in his throat, Jared stayed outside a moment longer. Then, in answer to a call, he strolled toward the light in the doorway, an impish grin spreading across his face.

CHAPTER NINE

Wednesday,
June 20th

*D*EAR *Hetty,*
I can hear Dr. Franklin as I'm writing, calling for daily prayer. He seems to be saying that only help from the heavens can guide this Convention now. I must admit, I see his point. No one agrees on anything. Poor Alexander Hamilton . . . he spent all day Monday and half of Tuesday speaking nonstop in favor of a strong national government. When he finished, no one said a word. Totally frustrated, he walked out. Uncle Thomas says he is going back to New York.

I'm certain you remember me telling you about Henry Blair. Well, my talks with him have raised my consciousness about the slavery issue in our new country. Henry is considering buying his freedom and staying in Philadelphia. It will be good to hear your opinions on the subject.

Do you know that if we couldn't talk and write to each other I think I'd burst? As always, I can't wait for our Sunday picnic. See you at our usual spot.

Your most obedient
servant,
Jared

Jared carefully tore the paper out of his ledger and folded it to fit into the envelope.

The sounds of heated debate continued to emerge from the East Room. Jared was fascinated by this war of egos, but because he was not actually present in the room, he could only picture for himself what was occurring. The pieces didn't always fit together. He would be disappointed if Alexander Hamilton came and went before he had a chance to talk with him, but his departure now seemed inevitable.

Grown men, Jared thought, supposedly working toward the same objective, should be able to resolve their differences more swiftly than this. His hope that the Convention would end by mid-July was slowly fading away.

In this second week of the Convention, Dayton seemed to be leaving with greater frequency. It dawned on Jared as he followed Dayton's movements that his pacing in the yard usually led to a conversation with Hetty, if she happened to be there. Either he was enticed by Hetty's beauty or wanted to appear in as many sketches as possible; either way, Jared was uncomfortable, and was angered by this obvious behavior.

His thoughts were interrupted by the thumping of canes. It seemed someone had finally said something to please the entire group. Just as he began to wonder on what issue a consensus might have been reached, the chamber door burst open, and once again, Dayton stormed out.

Cursing under his breath, he walked across the corridor and leaned against a pillar, his head cushioned by his forearm. Mr. Fry jumped up and gently closed the half-open door, at which point Dayton swung around and shouted, "I'll be going back in directly," dressing down poor Mr. Fry, who was only trying to perform his job. "You needn't stare so," he continued. "Haven't you ever seen someone angry before? I tell you, there are some pigheaded old men in that room who seem to care little about the opinion of the next generation."

He was pacing briskly now, taking six steps in one direction and six in the other. Jared was thinking that Dayton was the most pigheaded of the lot.

"I have better things to do with my time than spend a summer arguing with aged statesmen who act as though they and only they have the power to decide what is best for the country. The next time I am put in my place, I think I shall have no choice but to leave permanently. *That* would show those stuffy Virginians once and for all!"

He stopped pacing directly in front of Jared. "What's that book you have in your hand, Master Mifflin? Give it here. Let me see what it contains." His outstretched arm was waving about as he tried to coerce Jared to hand over his belongings. Jared would not oblige such a man, nor would he compromise Hetty. There were two more letters in the book ready to go.

"It's simply a journal I keep," Jared lied, quickly closing the book and stashing it in his satchel.

"Journal, you say? You are keeping a record of what you see and hear?" he screamed, sounding more and more like a maniac. "Certainly you must be aware that these proceedings are being kept secret from the public. I demand that you, as an employee of our group, take not one more notation, do you hear?" Dayton had begun to perspire, and his classic good looks were dissolving into creases of aggravation that lined his red face. "If you won't give me your journal I shall have to report this matter to Mr. Madison."

William, who had been standing behind a pillar, heard Dayton's demands and emphatically shook his head. With William's encouragement, Jared rose from his seat and confronted the rascal.

"I must say, Mr. Dayton, that this is not the first time I have witnessed your explosive personality, and I daresay it will not be the last. It is quite disagreeable to me, and I see no reason that I should have to turn anything over to you. Now, if you feel you have cause to complain further, be my guest. I am perfectly capable of explaining my writings to anyone. Do you plan to reenter the chamber? If not, I suggest you take leave of this building immediately."

Jared thought Dayton's puffy red face would explode. But, prepared for a further outburst, he did not allow himself to blink, or his stare to waver.

"I shall return to the East Room, if you please. But I warn you, you have not heard the last of me."

Mr. Fry, who had inched his way down to the farthest end of the bench, jumped up and, almost cowering, opened the door, thus helping to end the dreadful scene.

When the door closed behind Dayton, William cheered, "Bravo, bravo. Whatever it was that came over you, Jared, I am glad you put the lousy bloke in his place. Good job, old boy."

"It's not hard when you're dealing with a character as despicable as Dayton," Jared said with a bit of pride. "There is scuttlebutt going around that his only interest in serving at this Convention is his wanting to go down in history as being the youngest delegate. Not only does he have an awful temper, but he's just plain mean. You should see how he treated Henry at the Indian Queen. He can't stand Negroes, you know. The only thing he seems to have taken a liking to is Hetty."

"Hetty!" William responded. "C'mon, she's your girl."

"That she is, but I can't compete with this 'elder statesman,' who fancies himself to be some sort of gift to the republic! She's doing his portrait upon her father's suggestion. Hetty can create a sketch of someone in one or two sittings, but Dayton has managed to sit for her three or four times now. I tell you, William, I don't like it one bit."

"Well, if I were in your shoes, I'd figure out a way to escape from your family's social schedule a bit more. It seems that you better start taking your courting as seriously as you're taking this job!"

"I *have* managed to write several extra letters, anyway, and I've even found some envelopes. Do you think you could find some sealing wax before you deliver them this time?" Jared asked.

"Don't give it another thought," William answered, taking the folded paper and envelopes from Jared. "If you'll give these remedies to the doctor before noon," William said, handing over the pouch, "I'll be on my way."

After William had gone out the back door, Jared noticed Nehemiah Weaver approach his friend. The writer pointed to the letters in William's hand, but William simply shook his head. Stuffing the letters in his vest, he continued on his way. But Weaver kept pace with him.

It's now or never, Jared thought to himself. *I had no trouble confronting Dayton. Why not take on Weaver?* He told Mr. Fry that he would be at the back door should anyone need him, and quickly headed for his target.

"Mr. Weaver, I believe?" Jared asked just as he was about to cross Chestnut Street. "Nehemiah Weaver?"

"Yes, yes, that's me," the writer answered, looking at Jared with a hopeful expression.

"I'm Jared Mifflin, nephew of the State Assembly President and aide to James Madison."

"I know, I know, young man. I am most pleased that you care to speak with me. You are in an enviable position and no doubt have great information to share with an eager public. . . ."

Jared cut him off. "I wouldn't want you to misunderstand my intentions, Mr. Weaver, because I came not to divulge information, but to inform you that we wish you people from the newspapers not to linger in the hallways any longer. We also ask that you hold any stories you might be privy to until the delegates are ready to disclose their collective thoughts."

"I beg your pardon, lad," Weaver answered in a most condescending manner. "I've a job to do, just as you have. Might I remind you that I represent the most prestigious newspaper in all the thirteen colonies. It is, in fact, my duty to report, as best I can, the happenings behind those doors that you guard. Citizens, not as privileged as you I might add, are clamoring for information, and those demigods inside refuse to utter a word. The *Gazette* is receiving many letters complaining that we report nothing of the Federal Convention."

Jared could only think that he'd heard this once before from William, and in part he did have to agree. However, he was also aware that his loyalty was to Mr. Madison. "They have their reasons, and in due time, Mr. Weaver, they will release their facts and ideas." His voice grew stronger as he built to the finish. "Now please, honor my request and stay away from these grounds until you are welcome."

"You can keep me from your building, sir, but not from attempting to gather information from other sources. Good day," he said and, turning on his heels, he walked off in the direction of the Indian Queen.

What would his other sources be? Jared pondered, heading back to his post. It was not enough to simply bar him from the State House, Jared now realized. If he was really to do a thorough job providing security, he would have to figure out Weaver's other moves.

Surely he was after William because of his connection to Dr. Franklin. But William didn't know that much about the Convention itself. Of course, servants could overhear meetings at the local taverns. Was Weaver getting information from them? One way to find out would be to pay a call on Henry. The Indian Queen was the place most frequented by delegates.

He was glad when four o'clock came and the delegates departed. Just as he was ready to slip out, planning to put off his afternoon chores until the morning, Mr. Madison called to him.

"Jared! Are you still here?"

"Yes, sir," he replied. He walked hesitantly into the room.

"Come over here and look at this," Mr. Madison said. His eyes blazed as he threw several copies of the *Pennsylvania Gazette* across his desk. The headlines said:

GRAND CONVENTION
takes punitive action against
RHODE ISLAND

GREAT Diversity Among Members
At FEDERAL CONVENTION

Jared's heart was pounding. James Madison didn't know how hard he had worked all day at keeping the crowds away from the East Room. And Jared didn't feel like making excuses for himself. Instead he simply blurted out, "The Rhode Island story isn't even true!"

"Of course not," Mr. Madison retorted. "And to my knowledge not one delegate has let slip any information outside of these chambers. We have no choice, Jared, but to step up security measures and to have you take an even more rigorous role in dealing with these rascal writers."

"I already am doing more, sir. Just this afternoon I barred Nehemiah Weaver from these grounds, and I am in the process of tracking down other possible leaks. You must consider some of your own colleagues, Mr. Madison, if I may be so bold as to say so. Charles Cotesworth Pinckney and Robert Lansing both talk frequently to Mr. Weaver and other writers who linger in the yard. Did you ever consider that they might be using the newspapers for their own purposes?"

"I can't imagine Charles Pinckney being so indiscreet, Jared. He is the strength behind the compromise between the small and large states. But who knows," he sighed, removing his spectacles and rubbing his eyes, "perhaps he feels the need of support from the press. There's certainly nothing to stop these delegates from writing anonymous letters to editors. I must admit that I've written my fair share of letters to various newspapers when I have felt the need for the public to understand a political issue."

Jared realized the thought worried him. As the Convention continued to heat up, the possibility existed that those delegates who felt desperate might surreptitiously go to the press.

"Well, enough talk." He straightened up his desk and retrieved the printed materials that so distressed him. "I will be bringing this matter to the floor of the Convention on the morrow." Mr. Madison left the room, and Jared sat back, staring at Washington's massive chair. He looked at the sun painted on the back of it and couldn't help but wonder whether the sun would continue to shine on this new country.

Jared hurried home after work and excused himself the minute dinner was over. The alleyway leading to the stables at the Indian Queen was dark; the innkeeper had neglected to replace several lantern wicks. Nevertheless, Jared found his way. The large wooden doors creaked as he gently pried them open and squeezed through.

"Who's there?" Henry called out, peering over the railing from the hayloft.

"It's only me," Jared whispered. When his eyes adjusted to the darkness, he noticed that Henry was pulling on his breeches and realized he had probably been asleep.

"I got nothin' to keep me busy this evenin'," Henry explained, "and I got to catch up on my sleep. I been workin' every day and every night. Mistuh Baldwin's friends is talkin' and drinkin' and carryin' on somethin' fierce. I been carryin' trays up and down the stairs till all hours."

"I've been tired lately, too," Jared said, sitting down on a bale of hay. "I figure if they keep up this pace it'll all be over before we know it. I hope so anyway. I could do with some time off."

As soon as the words slipped off his tongue Jared wished he could retract them. He realized that Henry never had days or weeks off. "How have you been, Henry?" Jared asked. "I haven't laid eyes on you for about a week now. Do you ever have reason to deliver a message to Mr. Baldwin at the State House? It would be nice to see you there."

"No suh," Henry answered, "but I do take him out, and then I get to see the town." He had by this time climbed down the ladder and was sitting across from Jared on the large step of one of the carriages. "I did go over to the London Coffee House, though . . ."

"You did?" Jared asked in wonder. "And?"

"Just like the white men say, that place had one big auction goin' on. I'll bet there was a hundred men all waitin' to buy boys my age."

Jared could hardly believe his ears. "How did you get in?"

"It was hard. I sure didn't want them to think I was goin' to be up for sale. I ain't here for that, no way."

"That's for sure," Jared answered, finding the story both intriguing and horrifying.

"But I had seen a mighty beautiful servant girl when you and I was there before, and she just happened to be sortin' vegetables when I went back for the auction. She knew right away what I was there for and took me in the back way so I could see all I wanted for myself. It was real sad, Jared. There was brothers bein' sold to separate families. Only thing different between this auction and ones back home is that there weren't no ladies or girls bein' sold."

Jared sat in silence. Up until meeting Henry, he had felt that slavery—at least the crueler aspects of it—was a southern issue. Now Henry was proving him wrong.

"I'm sorry, Henry," he said softly, as if to apologize for all the people of Philadelphia. "I mean, it must have been terrible for you to watch such a thing."

"Yessuh," Henry admitted. "But I'm tryin' to see all I can for myself. I came north with Mistuh Baldwin to try out a new life. My mamma and poppa knows that I might be wantin' to stay up here."

There was another silence between the two of them. Finally Jared changed the subject. "The reason I stopped by, Henry, was to ask if you've seen a tall, broad redheaded man about—someone who looks like he's snooping, perhaps hanging around the rooms where some of the delegates meet at night."

Henry thought for a moment. "Does he have a mustache?" he

asked, drawing a big curved one on his lip with his fingers, "and a book?"

"Sounds like the man," Jared answered.

"I saw him in here two nights this week. Always right next to the tavern door . . . that's where Mistuh Baldwin and his friends sit most evenin's."

"Do you listen to what they say?" Jared asked cautiously.

"Uh, uh!" Henry answered, knowing that to eavesdrop got you into trouble. "But that there man could hear everythin' where he was sittin'. He even wrote things down as he ate."

"That's just what I thought was happening, Henry," Jared said, happy for the information and now aware of at least one leak. "Thank you! I'd best be getting home." Jared reached across to pat his friend's shoulder and rose to leave. "Hope you can get yourself some sleep, Henry."

He felt good as he walked home; he had some substantial news for Mr. Madison.

CHAPTER TEN

"LAST one to Gray's Ferry buys the first drink!" Jonathan shouted to his friends, leaping onto his horse and speeding away from the crowd that had gathered by the State House.

"Hey, wait for us!" Jared called as he mounted his horse Betsy, and chased Jonathan down Seventh Street. "Hold up at the corner, you hear, Jonathan?" he bellowed. "If it's a race you want, we'll begin properly at the starting point, fair and square."

"That's telling him," Ebin said, galloping up alongside Jared. Luke Rhoades was close behind him. When the four of them reached the corner of Seventh and Race streets, they trotted up the few blocks to the starting line. There were horse races here every weekend, but today the area was empty because of the Independence Day orations.

Jared felt like celebrating. Although the Convention itself was on the brink of disaster, fortunately little of it had to do with him. He had successfully stopped the leaks to the press, and Mr. Madison seemed more than pleased with his services.

"I'm always game for a race," Jared said to Jonathan as they rode side by side, "but what's the big hurry?"

"I just wanted to beat the crowd going out to the Bartram estate. I knew that if we hung around any longer *you* would get stuck being dutiful, and we'd never get out of there."

"I had wanted to hear General Washington's address!"

"So did I," Jonathan admitted, "but after seeing all those carriages lined up, I decided that we'd have more fun if we took the first ferry and spent our spare time at Gray's Tavern."

"Not bad thinking," Jared said gamely. It felt good to be frivolous for a change.

"All right then," Jonathan announced, "everyone line up, and we'll have ourselves a race."

"I'll be the starter," Luke volunteered uncharacteristically. He was usually so quiet that it was surprising to see him assert himself.

"Well, all right then," Jonathan agreed. "Get on with it!"

Luke called out, "On your mark, get set . . . go!"

They were off. It was a good two-and-three-quarter miles from Race to Broad Street, followed by the final stretch down Ferry Road. In no time at all they had clattered down the cobblestone city street and passed the point where it turned into a dirt road. The houses stopped abruptly at Ninth Street, and in their place were trees and fields. Jonathan, Ebin, and Luke maintained a three-horse lead at the one-mile marker.

Jared knew that Betsy was always slow to start and then quick at the finish. Once they passed Funk's Tavern he took out his whip, and as much as he hated to do it, gave Betsy one good swat. She took off at twice her current speed, her rhythm well-paced and her gait smooth. With the wind whistling in his ears, Jared could barely hear the sounds of the others. It seemed only moments before he and Betsy handily passed them all and were clearly out in front.

"See you at the ferry," Jared called over his shoulder.

When the entrance to the ferry was in sight, he pulled back on the reins, easing Betsy into a trot. "Nice work, girl," Jared said, leaning over to pat her as they proceeded down the gravel walk.

"It never fails, Mifflin," Jonathan said, coming up from behind. "Couldn't you lose once in a while!"

"It's all in good fun, my friend," Jared said, smiling. "At least you aren't the last."

Luke and Ebin brought up the rear. "I guess Luke and I buy the drinks," Ebin said. "There's no point in delaying—I know I could stand an orange shrub right now. How about the rest of you?"

There was a unanimous cheer. The ferry was docked, waiting for passengers, so they walked their horses aboard. Slowly the large old weather-beaten wooden craft creaked away from the shore to begin its short voyage to the south side of the Schuylkill River.

Two Negroes, one on either side of the raft, began chanting as, hand over hand, they pulled on the ropes that enabled the vessel to make the crossing.

Jared leaned against the fragile railing at the ferry's bow and gazed ahead. Gray's Tavern loomed larger and larger with every tug. He was very thirsty and his excitement about the day was mounting. "You're in for a busy day," he said to the ferry owner. "Some thirty-odd carriage loads of people are heading this way— should be here any time now."

"I hear General Washington's among them, lad," the ferryman answered. "Is that right?"

"That he is, along with Benjamin Franklin, James Madison, and every other important man in the country. I hope your vessel is seaworthy; you will be carrying a lofty crowd," Jared said, patting the railing and winking at the man.

"I'm mighty grateful for the news, young man. Gives my crew and me a little warning."

They gave the man a shilling each and led their horses to the tavern's hitching post. Moving quickly inside, Ebin placed an order for the group and sat down at the table overlooking the river. The rest followed.

"It sure feels good to be here," Jared said, loosening his collar and removing his jacket. He propped his feet up on a nearby bench.

"So tell us, what will become of this country, Jared?" Ebin inquired after he had taken a long drink from one of the tankards set down in front of them. "We hear you are privy to all sorts of things."

"And tell us what the general is like," Jonathan added.

"Which one?" Jared asked. "There are so many . . . General Hamilton, General Pinckney, General Washington, General Mifflin—"

"You know who I mean; Washington, of course."

"Well, I really only see him coming and going," Jared said, being careful not to give anything away. "And it's difficult to hear through those heavy doors. But you know, he was elected president of the Convention. I figure if they can't accomplish the job with a man like General Washington in charge, there will *never* be a Constitution."

Jonathan, easily bored with anything that smacked of seriousness, changed the subject. "I hear Bartram has planned quite a party today. Does anyone know who'll be there?"

"I assume you mean ladies and not delegates, isn't that right, Jonathan?" Ebin said with a laugh. "Well, Hetty Morris will surely be there," he continued with a grin. "I saw her back at the State House. I hope to catch her eye early on in the day."

Jared nearly choked on his second orange shrub. "She *is* awfully pretty," he said, recovering. "But just how do *you* plan to attract her? I mean, don't you think you're aiming a bit high?" Everyone laughed.

"She is fair game, isn't she?" Ebin challenged them. "I plan to fill her dance card before any of you get a chance."

"Oh, you do, do you?" Jared teased. "But what if I beat you to it?" He smiled at the thought that they'd soon know he'd won her heart.

"Knowing you, Jared," Jonathan interrupted, "you'll get yourself involved in a political debate and be unaware that the ball has even begun."

"You think so?" Jared said. He was amused at the conversation because he well knew that Hetty planned to reserve a good part of the evening for him. Their last three letters and their Sunday meetings had been full of plans for this evening.

"Enough about Hetty," Ebin finally said. "She's only one girl. Any guess as to who else is coming?"

"Governor Randolph's daughter, for one," Jared said. "He brought his entire family north for the summer. Rebecca's her name. She's really something!"

"Let us not overlook Mary and Elizabeth Mifflin," Jonathan said with a wink as Jared quickly looked around the table at his friends with a protective scowl.

Luke smiled shyly. "Any others?"

"I suppose Katherine Fitzsimmons will come, along with any other daughters that the Pennsylvania delegates might have lurking about!" Jared said. He couldn't believe how cavalierly he was talking about women. If Hetty could hear him she'd be appalled. "Oh, and there's one more sure bet," he added. "Herriot Pinckney."

"Here's to more than our share of pleasant company this evening," Ebin said, raising his tankard above the table in a toast.

They noticed out the window that the first ferry load of guests were disembarking.

"Bottoms up, men; we're off," Jonathan announced, gulping down the last of his drink and quickly heading for the door. "Unless, of course, you want to get mixed up in all that traffic!"

"Wait for me," Jared said, rising quickly after he noticed James Madison out of the corner of his eye. "I see duty heading my way."

The others joined Jared and Jonathan at the hitching post. "Giddap," they ordered in unison, and turned their horses in the direction of the Bartram estate.

There were several hours before the fox hunt. Mr. Bartram had ordered his fleet of coaches to wait at the tavern in order to transport the ladies and some of the older dignitaries to his estate. Many of those who planned to participate in the hunt brought their horses across the river with them. But with seventy or eighty guests to transport by water and land, Mr. Bartram had thoughtfully organized no formal activity until early afternoon.

The boys were greeted by the Bartram daughters, who eagerly

gave them a tour of the mansion and the grounds. After changing into their riding habits they lounged on the patio, awaiting the start of the hunt.

The estate bustled as coaches continued to drop guests at the front doors. Mrs. Bartram, very much at home overseeing such grand affairs, led the ladies inside to freshen up and take tea, while most of the men were ushered into guest chambers to change.

Servants scurried about assisting lost visitors, and even Henry, who had accompanied Abraham Baldwin for the day, was put to work helping out with the horses. The main house consisted of several grand public rooms and more than ten sleeping chambers. It was all quite merry, everyone being a good sport about sharing space and privy areas. Finally the appointed hour arrived and everyone assembled at the meet in front of the stables.

"Better get our mounts," Jared said to Jonathan and Luke, who were also riding. Joining the field, Jared counted at least thirty riders scattered about, their blue and brown jackets standing out against the lush backdrop of the estate. Hetty had offered to sketch the scene for him. Seeing her sitting to the side of the porch with her pad resting in her lap, Jared watched her drink in the action. Their eyes connected, and the moment was enough to make him want to be the first to spot the fox.

The anticipation was exhilarating. Jared wondered where the hounds would lead them—Mr. Bartram's huntsman had led the riders to believe the field would be directed into the unknown territory that surrounded the estate.

Just then the kennelman appeared with thirty-two hounds, eagerly tugging on their lines. Jared's heart skipped a beat as he gazed about. Who would have thought that someday he'd be riding the hunt with George Washington and James Madison? He found himself wishing his father could be there to share this moment. Glancing over at Jonathan and Luke, he was comforted to know that within the field there was a wide range of age and ability.

Mounted on one of Mr. Bartram's prize thoroughbreds, General

Washington looked more at home in his habit and top hat and more pleased with the day's events than Jared had ever seen him. The general was considered one of the country's keenest foxhunters, and it was because of his passion for the sport that Mr. Bartram had arranged a hunt so unusually late in the season.

After an initial greeting by Mr. Bartram, the huntsman raised the horn to his lips. The call was sounded, the hounds released, and the hunt was on. General Washington and James Madison, riding directly behind the staff, were well off by the time the younger members fell into a rhythm. Jared found himself riding parallel to Jona Dayton. He urged Betsy ahead and soon approached the first jump, a rather imposing rasper. Betsy cleared it comfortably, and Jared listened to the sounds of the horses as they thundered across the grounds in a loosely patterned unit, their hooves pounding against the hard earth. Ahead, the cry of the hounds indicated that they had picked up the scent. Across a broad meadow, up a steep embankment, and into a thick forest they rode. Trees, bushes, and undergrowth made it difficult to ride at an uninterrupted pace, and Jared couldn't help but admire the fox's instinctive cunning. He was aware of Jona Dayton's continued presence on his right no matter which direction Betsy moved.

They were approaching a narrow opening as Dayton called out, "On your right, Mifflin," his whip cracking across his horse's rump.

It was impossible for the two of them to make it through side by side. Jared quickly reined in Betsy in an effort to slow her down. Displeased with Jared's sudden decision, she unexpectedly threw her head and in so doing stepped slightly off balance. Jared was caught unaware and saw the low hanging branches too late.

Showing none of the respect so important to the sport, Dayton did not even slow to check on Jared. As Jared watched the brash young delegate follow the field, he brushed himself off and moved over to Betsy, who waited obediently nearby.

"We might not hear the 'Tally Ho!,' but I'd like to see it through

The hunt

to the end, old girl," Jared said. Replacing his derby, he gave Betsy a pat before placing his boot into the stirrup and pulling himself into the saddle.

"Giddap, Betsy," Jared urged with a smile crossing his face. "We've won one race today. I suppose I'd be in trouble with Jonathan and the others if we excelled in the hunt as well." Off they cantered, following the retreating pack.

Within fifteen minutes they caught up with the field excitedly gathered at a standstill. The hounds were wildly dancing about a hole at the base of a tree. The fox had gone to ground. Pleased with the dogs and the ride, the huntsman signaled the conclusion of the hunt.

As the whippers-in worked with the hounds, Jared dismounted and led Betsy over to a small pond for some well-deserved refreshment.

"Congratulations, James, on a grand ride!" he heard Uncle Thomas exclaim. Jared turned and saw the two men riding side by side. Jared waved at them, thinking that James Madison was as serious about the hunt as he was about the Convention. He hoped the man was aware of the integral role he was playing in this country's development. *If anyone deserves praise*, Jared concluded, *it's James Madison.*

Once back at the mansion and changed, Jared found his friends— in the company of several young ladies—gathered under a tall oak tree. Greeting the group, he noticed William under the tree along with the others.

"William, where did you come from?" Jared asked, surprised.

"We were just introducing ourselves," Jonathan piped up. "Quite a novelty, don't you think? Having an Englishman at an Independence Day party?"

Everyone laughed at Jonathan's cool sarcasm, and Jared quickly revealed that William was an aide to Dr. Franklin, thereby giving his friend immediate importance.

"What sort of work do you do?" Ebin asked. "I don't suppose

you help him bundle up thunder and lightning?" he teased, referring to Dr. Franklin's experiments with electricity.

William wasn't sure how to answer such a question now that Jared had glorified his status. For once he was speechless, and he looked helplessly at Jared, who quickly put in, "He performs many of the same sort of duties I do for Mr. Madison." And cleverly changing the subject, he added, "Why are we dallying—isn't there something planned for the afternoon?"

"We're going fishing," Jonathan said.

"These ladies have challenged us to a game of croquet," Luke continued, "but we'd already planned a fly-fishing contest."

"Is there some reason why we can't do both?" Jared suggested. "If we head for the river now, we can be back by teatime, after which we'll be ready to accept the challenge."

"Well planned," Hetty piped up, gazing mischievously over at the croquet game set up on the lawn. "I suggest we use the time to prepare ourselves for the competition. We do want to give these boys a run for their money, if that is, they don't drop from exhaustion first," she teased, looking boldly at Jared.

Katherine Fitzsimmons, who appeared to be as headstrong as Hetty, agreed, and they wandered off.

"We've certainly got our afternoon challenges lined up, don't we?" Jonathan asked. "We'd best head straight for the river and see how many fish we're able to hook."

Jonathan, Ebin, and Luke led the group, as Jared and William followed a few paces behind.

"How did you manage to get the day off?" Jared whispered.

"About time, wouldn't you say? I've been working three months without a day to call my own! It's too bad your friend Henry can't go fishing with us."

"So you've seen him, too," Jared said.

"Sure, he's been in and around the stables most of the day. With so many men bringing their horses over for the hunt, Bartram put the word out that he needed extra livery boys. I hardly recognized him in that white powdered wig and fancy jacket. Maybe after everyone's arrived we can rescue him for a swim in the river."

"We'll see," Jared said, his voice trailing off as he recalled the way his friends had reacted when they saw him in Henry's company a few weeks earlier.

"C'mon, everyone!" Jonathan bellowed, motioning from the riverbank.

William and Jared took a pole from the boat house. "You go ahead," Jared encouraged. "Let's see what you can do."

Jared found a large flat rock to lean against. It had already been a full day, and the best was yet to come. The evening ahead held such promise. . . .

The rippling water lulled Jared into a daydream. He ceased to be aware of the others, who were searching the shadowy current for trout. An hour or so passed that way. Then the stillness was broken by a frantic voice calling from the top of the bank.

"Jared! Jared Mifflin! Are you down there? Can you hear me?" The voice became more and more agitated. Jared bolted upright when he realized that it was Hetty. Jumping to his feet, he ran up the hill.

"It's your friend Henry," she screamed. "He's hurt!"

The third trout was hanging on William's line when he heard what Hetty was saying. Dropping his rod, he followed Jared at a run.

Jared and William reached the crest of the hill in time to see Hetty burst into tears. "Back there . . . beside the house . . . Henry's lying helpless . . . he looks dead," she cried. She pointed in the direction of the mansion, her hand shaking as her tears turned to sobs.

"Lying? What do you mean?" Jared asked, grabbing her by the shoulders. "Hetty, slow down. You're not making any sense."

"Yes, she is," William interrupted. "Henry's been injured, and it sounds like he's unconscious."

The three started across the broad meadow, Jared torn between keeping pace with William and staying by Hetty's side to comfort her. With William well ahead they cut through Mr. Bartram's formal gardens. Several servants had gathered around Henry's limp body, and a few gentlemen were escorting ladies away. First William, then Jared and Hetty pushed through the group standing idly by.

"He's alive, isn't he, Jared?" Hetty asked, holding her hand over her mouth.

William was already kneeling beside the body, feeling for a pulse. "Henry, Henry, do you hear me?" he pleaded.

The ground beneath Henry's head was bloodstained. When William removed the wig and saw the gash, he gasped. "Get a doctor! Is there one in the party?"

"I know one," Jared said. Removing his jacket, he said, "Prop his head up with this. And Hetty, go get some cool water and towels . . . and a blanket, too." He immediately left to find Dr. James McHenry, one of the delegates from Maryland.

Knowing that many of the delegates had been anxious to tour the Bartrams' collection of plants, Jared hurried toward the botanical gardens.

"Jared, my boy," a voice called to him from somewhere behind the maze of shrubs. Mr. Bartram had designed a series of pathways among the well-clipped shrubbery. Once inside the maze it was difficult to find the way out.

"Uncle Thomas, is that you?" Jared called out.

"Yes, over here," he answered.

"Where's here?" Jared asked, frustrated now at the ridiculousness of such a place. "A friend of mine has been badly injured, kicked in the head by a horse. Do you know where Dr. McHenry is?"

"He's with his fellow Marylanders. I think they went to inspect the farmlands," Uncle Thomas answered. "Mr. Bartram has a most unique way of forcing his fruit trees into full growth long before they are normally harvested."

"Uncle Thomas, I'm afraid I don't have time right now . . ."

After starting off in four different directions, Jared finally found his way out of the maze.

He ran toward the fields, which seemed hauntingly distant. There, amidst the rows of pear trees, was a group of men deep in discussion. And Dr. McHenry was among them.

"Excuse me, Doctor," Jared said breathlessly, interrupting Mr. Bartram's lecture. "We need your services," he continued. "Someone has been injured."

"Can't it wait, young man?" Dr. McHenry asked. "I'm sure nothing too serious could occur on such a fine day."

"But sir, it's a friend of mine. He is unconscious by the stables. He needs treatment immediately, I'm certain. Please," Jared pleaded. The fact that he had to beg the man angered him.

"All right, then, all right. If you'll excuse me, gentlemen, I should be back shortly."

"This way, sir, and hurry please," Jared said. He ran ahead, hoping the doctor would make an effort to match his stride.

When they arrived at the scene, Henry had not moved. Hetty was applying a cool cloth to his forehead and around the gash.

"A Negro?" Dr. McHenry remarked. "You called me away just for him?" Bending down he grumbled, "Let's see what we have." He turned Henry's head to one side. "Three inches closer to the temple and he'd be gone. Move him to the barn." His voice was void of any emotion. Jared found himself hating this man.

"Why not the main house?" Hetty asked indignantly. "The barn is hot and dirty. Shouldn't he be put to bed?"

"The barn is good enough for him," Dr. McHenry replied. "Besides, Mrs. Bartram is planning for the ball, and we don't want to upset her plans with this. Get me some smelling salts and bandages. We'll try to fix him up. Bad concussion, that's all it is," the doctor continued.

Jared and William lifted Henry and carried him into the barn. They searched for a cool, dark corner away from the flies and animals and laid him across several bales of hay.

William looked at Jared. He didn't have to say a word for Jared to know what he was thinking: *The rich get taken care of, while all others try to survive on their own.* His eyes said it all.

"Come on, Henry," Jared said, reaching out to touch his friend's shoulder. "Come on," he pleaded. "Open your eyes."

Hetty ran in. "Here are the smelling salts." Dr. McHenry uncorked the bottle and placed it under Henry's nose.

"Wake up. Wake up. Please," Jared said quietly.

The moments seemed endless. First Henry's eyes flickered, and then they opened.

"Henry!" William and Jared said in unison. Only William noticed the doctor wander away.

"Where am I?" he asked, and they knew Henry was going to be all right.

CHAPTER ELEVEN

WHEN darkness began to envelop the stately stone mansion, torches lit the great lawn, and candles could be seen flickering in every window.

Jared was amazed to discover that the Mifflins were seated at dinner not only with General Washington, but with Hetty and her parents as well.

Halfway through the meal the general proposed a toast: "The United States! May the Union be strengthened and preserved."

"Here, here," everyone responded, clinking glasses and smiling at each other. *A novelty for the delegates*, Jared thought as he observed the scene. His eyes met Hetty's and a chill shot down his spine.

Hetty looked away and engaged William Samuel Johnson in conversation. Jared couldn't help but notice how at ease she was in any situation. Taking his cue from her, he began inquiring of Mrs. John Rutledge, who was on his right, as to how she was enjoying her summer away from Charleston. Jared questioned her about southern plantation living, and she was eager to respond. Although what Mrs. Rutledge was saying did interest him, he kept one ear on the other conversations around him—issues concerning the western lands, the Indian problem, and, of course, slavery. Perhaps General Washington well knew what he was doing when he suggested this dinner party. It was odd to see these men talking calmly about the very same issues they shouted about in the East Room.

The airy harpsichord music coming from the ballroom made Jared anxious for dinner to be over and the dancing to begin. He involved himself less and less in conversation, concentrating instead on the way the general had asked for seating to be arranged. Each man at the general's table was a key figure in the debate over representation. If the general and Mr. Madison could enlist the good graces of these men tonight, perhaps the deadlocked Convention would begin to move again.

That's why General Washington is unusually jovial—Jared thought, *flattering the guests, and particularly their wives. I've never seen him quite so outgoing.* He was pleased with himself for figuring out the man's scheme.

Several more rounds of toasts and two more courses followed before the butler delivered the message to each table that Mr. and Mrs. Bartram requested their guests' presence for dancing in the ballroom.

As groups of people made their way toward the ballroom, Jared noticed Ebin and Jonathan looking about, probably—he thought—for Hetty.

"Shall we, Miss Morris?" Jared said quickly, with a formal bow. She replied simply by slipping her arm into his, and together they glided into the ballroom. The setting was perfect for a romantic evening. The hanging prisms on the three crystal chandeliers cast twinkling lights across the ceiling, creating a starlit effect for those dancing below.

Jared winked at Ebin, who was now scanning the room in search of a partner. Jared motioned toward Herriot Pinckney, then took Hetty's arm and led her to the floor.

Her sapphire-blue satin gown sparkled in the candlelit room. It was a wonderful coincidence that Jared's blue and white jacket matched her ensemble completely.

"Finally," Jared said quietly as they bowed and curtsied to each other, "we are together for all to see."

"Ah yes," Hetty answered, as they moved around in the circle, "but perhaps not for long. I do have a dance card, you know—it could readily be filled up."

"Yes, but you see, I intend to scratch my name on every line the moment this minuet is over," Jared replied.

"But, Jared, aren't you being a bit unfair? After all, two of your friends spoke to me while you were off hunting; they and several others have asked for a dance or two. I could hardly say no," she teased.

"Well, I suppose I should share the loveliest girl here; I'll give up one or two dances, but that's all."

"Why, Jared Mifflin." She blushed. "I don't believe I've ever seen you so bullish—at least not where ladies are concerned."

"Not ladies, Hetty, just one lady; and this won't be the last time you witness this side of me. I intend, by the end of the evening, to let everyone know just whose girl you are."

"My cheeks are on fire!" she said with embarrassment.

"Well," he countered, "you look even more radiant; may I have another dance?"

She smiled at him as a waltz began, allowing her small frame to rest in his strong hand. They whirled about the highly polished dance floor, unaware that anyone else was sharing the music that seemed to be playing just for them.

When the waltz ended, Jared reluctantly stepped away from Hetty and clapped for the musicians. "I suppose not even the general could do anything about the heat, though he did think of everything else. Would you care for some punch?" he asked. Hetty nodded with a smile.

"Now don't you get your dance card filled while I'm away," he cautioned and returned the smile.

"I'll try my best," she replied, dipping her chin behind her fan.

By the time Jared reached the punch bowl and glanced back toward the dance floor, Hetty was surrounded by young men, most of them his friends. *Oh, well,* Jared mused. *I might as well let Jonathan and Luke have their moment with Hetty.* As he sipped his punch, he looked around the room at the other ladies, wondering who he might ask to dance. When one of the black servants caught his eye, Jared thought of his friend lying in the barn. "Oh, my!" he said aloud. "I've forgotten all about Henry." Heading immediately toward the door he deposited his cup at a nearby mahogany table and walked briskly into the dark night. *I haven't seen him for hours,* Jared thought, trying to reckon with his feelings of guilt.

The huge Bartram barn was pitch-black. Jared couldn't see or hear a thing as he entered. He stood motionless until he got his bearings and then proceeded down the center, his feet rustling the hay that was spread across the floor.

"Who is it?" a startled voice sounded from nearby.

Jared turned and saw Henry's figure, sitting upright, his body silhouetted against the hay. He was sipping water from a mug.

"How are you feeling?" Jared asked as he approached. "You look better."

"My head hurts real bad," Henry said, "but I feel bettuh than before. Your white people's music keeps puttin' me to sleep. You sure could stand somethin' with more spirit," Henry said, obviously joking.

Jared could tell from Henry's attitude that he was going to be fine. They talked a few minutes more before Jared reluctantly allowed thoughts of the ballroom to beckon him.

"Can I bring you anything, Henry?" he asked picking a piece of straw from under his jacket.

"No, Jared," Henry answered. "Just make sure Mistuh Baldwin don't forget me when the party's ovuh."

"I'll remind him," Jared said. *Did he finally call me by name?* Jared thought as he walked back toward the mansion. It seemed very comfortable, even natural, that Henry had become a part of his new circle of friends. A smile crossed Jared's face.

By the time he returned, Hetty was nowhere to be found. Jared noticed Katherine Fitzsimmons, standing out in the crowd in her striking pink ball gown, and asked her to dance. As they glided about the room, he scanned the crowd, wondering where Hetty could have gone to. Aunt Sarah was standing off to the side and smiled at him as he and Katherine waltzed by. After returning Katherine to her friends, Jared gallantly escorted his aunt onto the dance floor. Then chasing the suitors away from his cousins, he devoted the next two dances to Elizabeth and Mary, so that he could catch up on their evenings.

There was so much glamour to the evening, heightened, he supposed, by the presence of General Washington. The Bartrams had hired Philadelphia's finest string ensemble, and the public rooms were festooned with garlands of honeysuckle and laurel. As he saw Mary back to her group of young friends he turned once again to look for Hetty. Servants had uncorked numerous bottles of champagne, and glasses were being passed around the room. Jared scooped two glasses off a tray and continued looking about for Hetty. Not finding her in the ballroom he casually made his way toward the patio, stopping just short of the French doors. There he saw Jona Dayton, his back toward the ballroom, talking to Hetty. She was barely visible from where Jared stood, and by the way Dayton was positioned, legs apart, facing her, it seemed to Jared as though Hetty was trapped in conversation without hope of escape.

Taking a deep breath, Jared gulped down one of the glasses of champagne and marched over to the two of them.

"Good evening, Mr. Dayton, Hetty," Jared said, nodding his head in respect. "I haven't had the pleasure all evening."

"Good evening, Mifflin," Dayton answered curtly. "I was just telling Miss Morris that her portraits are so exquisite she should consider showing them in New York City. Don't you agree?"

"I really have no desire to display my work that way, Mr. Dayton," Hetty answered quickly, "although I am most humbled by your suggestion."

Jared was becoming impatient with this small talk, hoping the amenities would conclude. There was an awkward silence. "I do believe, Hetty, that I have the next dance," he said finally.

"I can't imagine you would, Mifflin," Dayton responded, "as you seem to have had most of Miss Morris's dances this evening."

"I do declare," Hetty said to Jared, glancing at her card, "you are indeed right."

"Shall we then?" Jared suggested, extending his arm.

"Not so fast, Master Mifflin. I do want to affix my name to this lady's card before you once again whisk her away."

Hetty held it out for him to see. "I'm afraid it's filled for the remainder of the evening, Jona," she said sweetly.

"Then perhaps Master Mifflin would grant me one of his dances," Jona said, glaring at Jared.

"Afraid not tonight, Dayton," Jared answered, leading Hetty toward the ballroom. "Perhaps some other evening."

"Jared," Hetty said, scolding him as they began to dance, "you are a naughty one, putting Jona in his place like that. Why, I actually feel rather sorry for him."

"Hetty, you've heard the expression 'May the better man win.' I told you at the beginning of this evening that my intentions would be clear to everyone by the night's end, and I intend to remain true to my word."

"You needn't worry about Jona," Hetty said. "He's such a child, really—sometimes the bully, sometimes the show-off, and sometimes the scoundrel. But he's harmless."

Jared grinned. *She never ceases to amaze me,* he thought. *And if there's one thing I well know, it's that Hetty can take care of herself.* His grip on her back became firmer as though to show her how proud of her he was. He had never experienced such exhilaration—the intensity of the feeling between them was electric. Neither said another word, and Jared could only guess how many dances transpired before the ensemble's next break.

"Shall we get some fresh air?" Jared suggested, already leading her through the French doors. They walked in silence for a few moments until Jared said, "Hetty, it's so good to be together. I feel we're together all the time, just through my letters, but actually being here with you is wonderful. Do you know that my very last thoughts each evening go onto paper to you?"

"You are a silly, Jared Mifflin," Hetty teased. "Why, you haven't sent me that many letters," she said. "Perhaps that's why I enjoy them so—they come infrequently, but they're rich in detail."

Jared stopped. "Infrequently? Hetty, don't joke with me. In the past few weeks I have written to you at least once a day."

"Jared, you don't have to be defensive. I know very well how long your days are, and when you get home you must just collapse. It doesn't matter one bit to me how often you write. It's what you say that means so much."

"But Hetty, you don't understand. I really have been writing to you every day, and William Ellsworth has been delivering the letters!" he said, raising his voice.

"Shhh, Jared," she said, putting her fingers to his lips. "People can hear you. Besides, why clutter up such a perfect evening with something that can be discussed later?"

She slipped her hand through his arm, and they walked down the path. The ensemble began a minuet, but neither of them was interested in going back to the ballroom.

"Jared?"

"Yes," he answered, his voice sounding far away as he tried to decipher the mystery of the letters.

"Isn't the moon just beautiful? Look, over there," she said, pointing her finger toward the sky, "it keeps peeking out from behind those dark clouds."

"So it does," Jared answered, staring at Hetty rather than the moon.

She turned and looked into his eyes, the veiled moonlight softly illuminating her face. Neither of them spoke. Hetty reached out and held Jared's hands in hers.

"Will you kiss me?" she asked softly.

"What was that?" Jared asked, hardly able to believe his ears.

"I said, kiss me . . . please." She was smiling gently and did not take her eyes from his. He paused a moment, tilted her tiny face in his hands, and obliged.

Almost as soon as the evening began, it was over. When the grand clock chimed twelve times, the tired guests stood together and joined in the singing of "My Days Have Been So Wondrous Free." Then it was time for the long trip home.

"Jared, over here!" Uncle Thomas's hoarse voice could be heard above the throngs of party-goers making their way toward the carriages.

"How could he see us?" Jared whispered to Hetty. The two were lingering by the edge of the patio and were nearly the last ones to make their way to the carriages.

"You best go," Hetty said, her voice so sweet and sad that it took all the discipline Jared could muster to take his hand from hers.

Looking at her as he turned to go, he said, "See you in a few days, Hetty. You have made this one of the perfect nights of my life."

"Our carriage is over there," Uncle Thomas said impatiently when Jared joined him. "If we hurry we'll beat the crush at the ferry. Get Betsy and tie her up to the back next to Beau."

"Yes, sir," Jared said wearily, feeling jarred by Uncle Thomas's impatience.

By the time he had dragged Betsy back the carriage was full, not only with family members but with Benjamin Franklin as well. "Hop up back," Uncle Thomas directed. "The doctor and I are deep in conversation, and the girls have already fallen asleep on Aunt Sarah's lap."

"William!" Jared exclaimed as he climbed up onto the cumbersome perch. "What are you doing here?"

"I go where the doctor goes," he answered.

"Of course, how foolish of me," Jared answered, finding himself talking louder and faster than usual. The frivolity of the evening had not worn off. He leaned back and braced himself for the jolt that always came with the carriage's first movements, and thought of Hetty. His head was bursting with sights and sounds and smells of the evening.

"So, tell me," he said, turning to William and patting his friend's knee, "did you enjoy your day off? I stopped in to see Henry during the night. He seems much improved," Jared continued, "but I suggested to Mr. Baldwin that he have our physician, Dr. Rush, see him when they get back to town."

The carriage jiggled up and down, jolting their bodies against one another each time it hit a rut. Jared was feeling dizzy—from the wine and champagne, he supposed—but not even that dampened his spirits.

"You think a doctor would see someone at this hour?" William asked sarcastically. "Especially a Negro? You must be joking."

"I am not," Jared asserted. "Dr. Rush is dedicated to his profession. Everyone knows he's at the dispensary night and day."

"If he's a physician, he must be a man of means, is he not?" William asked.

"True," Jared sighed, hoping that William wasn't leading up to one of his discourses on rich versus poor.

"Look, Jared," he said, "since I've arrived in this city . . . in this country, come to think of it . . . I've witnessed one instance after another where the lower classes get the bad lot. Take the party we just attended, for example. Nothing stopped because Henry was injured. If it hadn't been for you and Hetty he might never have received treatment. Allow me now to mention Dr. McHenry who is, I believe, one of your precious delegates."

Jared realized he was being talked into a corner.

"The Constitution that *he* is helping to write is supposed to be about liberty and freedom, correct?" When William received no response from Jared he continued, "As far as I can see, McHenry cares for personal liberty all right—for himself and not for anyone else. Certainly not for Negroes."

"All right! All right! I have to agree with you. But he's only one man," Jared argued. "You're generalizing once again. What do you know of the others?"

"I don't *know* anything," William said, exasperated. "I just know what I feel."

Jared wasn't sure how to respond.

"Did you have a good time at the ball?" William continued.

"Sure," Jared said, smiling as he thought of dancing with Hetty. "Where were you?" He became aware that he hadn't seen William all night.

William laughed. "That's funny, Jared. Where was I? I couldn't go. I'm a servant, remember? I'm not fit to be dancing with fancy ladies and gentlemen. Anyway, I didn't have the proper clothes."

"What did you do?" Jared asked, feeling as though someone had hit him in the stomach.

"I took my supper with the other servants and watched the dancing from the far end of the patio. You call that personal liberty and freedom? I must say one thing I've learned," William spoke angrily, "if I stay in this country, and if I can make myself a pile of money, I may then be able to buy myself some freedom. In that way I'm more fortunate than Henry."

Jared couldn't believe that he hadn't given William a thought once during the evening's festivities. So intent was he on beating his friends and Jona Dayton to Hetty's side that everything else ceased to be important. He had thought of no one but himself. Was he any different than Dr. McHenry?

As the carriage crossed the river on the ferry, the two young men sat in silence.

"So what did you do after the croquet match?" Jared asked.

"I went to sit with Henry," William answered. "Good thing, too, because except for Mr. Baldwin, no one had come out to bring him water or anything. It gave me a chance to get to know him better. We hadn't talked much the night of Dr. Franklin's dinner."

"Did he tell you about his plan to stay up north?" Jared asked.

"Yes, we talked about that. But you know what, Jared? Henry seems to be seeing much the same things that I am. I know you don't agree with us, but according to Henry there seem to be just as many people in Pennsylvania who judge a person on the basis of color as there are in Georgia. Henry says a slave is a slave. You can't move away from it—at least not in the colonies. Besides, Mr. Baldwin seems like one of the nicer men working on this Constitution. Henry's probably better off with him than in a paying job where he's treated badly."

"Hey, you two," Uncle Thomas called out the window. "Are you still awake? We're almost there."

They were nearing the Franklin home. Jared said good night to William. And as the carriage pulled away, he promised himself to think about what had been said. Jared wanted to find answers to William and Henry's problems. He leaned his head back against the carriage and let his thoughts drift to Hetty, confused because he felt guilty and happy at the same time. Then his thoughts collided as he drifted off to sleep for the rest of the ride.

Jared was relieved to be heading for the Mifflin country home. The carriage rocked back and forth, its wheels catching in the ruts that were always present on these back roads. Although he had grown accustomed to the constant action of the city, he found there was no better place to think than at the farm. And after all that had transpired the day before at the Bartrams', he needed his long weekend to sort things out.

Jared felt the expected thrill as the carriage made its final turn and wound through the archway of trees that led to the stone farmhouse. There were so many memories connected to this place—some real, some imagined. This was the home to which he had been delivered after his sisters and then his mother died. Aunt Sarah had thought it best to bring him into an environment similar to the one he had been forced to vacate. And today, as he gazed out the carriage window at the lush greenery and healthy gardens, Jared realized once again that he was a country boy at heart. Despite the fact that he had, for the most part, grown up in the bustling city of Philadelphia, his roots, his values, even his soul were firmly rooted in the land. *That's why I think more clearly out here,* Jared said to himself.

The carriage came to an abrupt halt by the front door, where Tildie and Charles, the Mifflins' country servants, waited to greet them. Jared looked into their faces with a new perspective.

"Well, well, well, here we are. Welcome to Riverside," Uncle Thomas said, helping James Madison out of the carriage. More often than not Uncle Thomas arrived at the country house with guests in tow. Jared wished that this particular weekend, the guest didn't have to be his employer.

There was a good deal of hustle and bustle as the girls and Aunt Sarah ran off to unpack, and Uncle started giving orders. "You shall have all the peace and quiet due you this weekend," he added. "Charles, show Mr. Madison to the guest quarters, and have Jim and the others unpack the coaches."

Jared had little trouble slipping away. He headed for a nearby stream, where as a young boy he had spent hours looking for frogs, digging up worms, and fishing. It was his hideout.

William, William, William, he thought as he strolled across the meadow. He couldn't get their conversation out of his head. This time William's directness had hit him squarely between the eyes. Jared was still upset that he could have been insensitive enough to lose himself in the evening and not even notice William's absence.

He picked up a handful of flat stones and began skipping them, one by one, into the stream. *Here I am,* he thought, *working loyally for the Constitutional Convention, actually thinking that I'm making a contribution to a worthy cause, and suddenly I begin to see the leaders of our country in a different light. Are they really striving for freedom? And whose freedom?* He reflected on Dr. McHenry's treatment of Henry, William's "place" at the ball, and Jona Dayton's prejudice. *Perhaps it is because these men* are *thinking about their own interests, rather than those of the country that the Convention seems to be facing such troubles.*

He pulled the worn copy of *Common Sense* out of his pocket. Turning to one of his favorite phrases, he read aloud:

We fight not to enslave but to set a country free and to make room upon the earth for honest men to live in.

That passage made his mind race to Massachusetts and to William's uncle in prison. Why had he been put in jail? What could a humble farmer have done to deserve such a punishment? *It doesn't make sense,* he thought, *that our new nation wouldn't support farmers.*

The stream, rippling as it washed over the rocks, temporarily soothed his troubles. But his mind soon turned toward William once more, and how he had had no concern for his friend once the ball began.

Jared walked along the water's edge, thinking that for the first time Paine's phrase actually had a pointed meaning for him: *These were the times that tried men's souls—that was for sure! If I hope to be one-half the man my father wanted me to be, I must follow my conscience and act upon it.*

He headed back to the farm.

"Where ever have you been hiding, my boy?" Uncle asked as Jared approached the porch. "Mr. Madison and I were just questioning Aunt Sarah as to your whereabouts."

Jared had hoped his absence would go unnoticed. He couldn't help but think about how much privacy and time alone he'd have once he went off to the university in the fall.

"Come. Come," Uncle Thomas insisted, jumping up and grabbing another white wicker rocker for Jared. Getting comfortable in the chair, Jared tucked the book into his jacket pocket, though not before Mr. Madison's curiosity was piqued.

"What have you there?" he asked. "I'm always interested in what people are reading."

"Well, sir, no doubt you've read and reread this one," Jared said, placing the book on the table.

James Madison retrieved it. "Ah yes, indeed," he said, flipping through the pages. "*Common Sense*—wonderful piece of writing. Paine has a way with words, don't you agree, Thomas?"

Jared's uncle nodded but said nothing.

"Do you two know that this book has sold more copies than any other publication in the colonies?"

"No, sir," Jared answered, "but I'm not surprised."

"Good thoughts in here," Madison added as he leafed through the pages.

"Now here's one:

Now is the seed time of continental union, faith and honor. The least fracture now will be like a name engraved with the point of a pin on the tender side of a young oak.

"And this is a favorite of mine:

The sun never shone on a cause of greater worth. This is not the affair of a city, a country, a province or a kingdom, but of a continent—of at least one eighth part of the habitable globe.

"You know, Thomas," he said, "Mr. Paine's thoughts are as pertinent now, as we struggle to formulate the Constitution, as they were when we fought to become a nation."

"It's an interesting point that you make, James," Uncle Thomas agreed without adding his usual commentary.

"If that is so," Jared began, "then mightn't it behoove your delegates to take into consideration the needs of the common man?"

"I'm not sure I follow you, son," Mr. Madison said.

"Well, it's just that I've been struck by the fact that most of the delegates are wealthy and powerful, and that they've been so for years. Do you suppose such a group is capable of formulating a document that takes every man into consideration?"

"Every man?" Uncle Thomas asked, the edge of his voice indicating that Jared seemed to be overstepping the boundaries permitted a young man when speaking with his elders.

"Yes, sir," Jared answered with confidence and authority. "While you men have been shut in behind the great doors of the East Room with your philosophies, thoughts, and special interests, I've been standing outside the door, keeping the commoners out and wondering how many of you have ever walked in their shoes."

"I beg your pardon!" Uncle Thomas said. "And what do you know of this so-called commoner you talk of? Aunt Sarah and I have taken great pains to surround you with fine things and the finest people in our city."

"Ah yes, Uncle, of course you have. But my job at the State House has broadened my horizons. I have come to know others that I might never have mixed with had it not been for this Convention."

"So?" Uncle said, making Jared's blood boil.

But he continued coolly, "Would you believe I've come to know a slave? He's from Georgia and has accompanied Mr. Abraham Baldwin to the Convention."

"A slave!" Uncle Thomas said in disbelief. "Why ever would you fraternize with the help, my boy? How can you communicate with such a person? Slaves can't even speak proper English."

"Well, Henry does. He's been educated and is even capable of earning himself a proper job. That is, if the law permitted such a thing. My work has taken me to all sorts of places I normally would not frequent, Uncle. I've been witness to several ugly scenes where some delegates have been less than cordial toward Negroes, for example. I would assume that the issue of slavery is one you are considering in the Constitution, is it not?"

"Well, that's a tricky one," Mr. Madison replied.

"But, sir, I'm sure you agree that in a free country they deserve respect at the very least. After all, my friend Henry says that over five thousand of them fought in the Revolution. Don't they deserve some sort of recognition in your document?"

"Jared," Uncle Thomas interrupted, "have you forgotten your manners? It's a bit presumptuous of you to advise Mr. Madison."

"No, no, Thomas," Mr. Madison said, "the boy is bright, and he makes a good point. Perhaps the Convention is going around in circles because we haven't taken time to look beyond our own lofty ideals. You speak with some common sense," he said, turning back to Jared and smiling at his pun. "Go on and tell us what else you have discovered."

Feeling as though he had passed a major school examination, Jared continued, "The other citizen I worry about is the farmer."

Uncle Thomas raised his eyes to the ceiling, clearly exasperated.

"I've been meaning to ask: What did happen in Massachusetts, sir, that put hundreds of farmers in prison? I can't imagine our country surviving without farms and the men who work them."

"They couldn't pay their taxes!" Uncle Thomas snapped. "A man must make a contribution to the common good, farmer or merchant."

"But it is a bit more complicated than that, Thomas," Mr. Madison cut in, seemingly anxious to speak on this issue. "You are referring to Shays's Rebellion, I believe, and coincidentally, that was one of the very incidents that hurried the process of the Convention along. Let me explain: The wealthy merchants of Boston wanted only to use specie, or metal currency, and refused to accept paper money from farmers in payment for their loans. As a result, hundreds of farmers were dispossessed and not only lost their farms but also their right to vote. With no strong government to back them, the farmers took up their rifles and meant to take over the Massachusetts courthouse buildings. Unfortunately for them, the state militia squelched their efforts, and most of them were sent off to prison."

So that's what happened to William's uncle, Jared thought. "Will the Constitution remedy the situation?" he asked.

Mr. Madison answered, "We are trying to create laws to make taxation and representation fair to all men."

"I suppose I'm taking this all a bit personally, sir," Jared said looking at his uncle, "but my father was a farmer. It occurred to me that had he lived I would have been brought up a common man and might have seen my own father thrown into debtors' prison as well. You know, Thomas Paine's great popularity is due, I think, to the fact that he speaks to everyone. I hope the Constitution will, too."

"That's my hope as well, Jared," Mr. Madison said, now sitting back in his chair and nursing his Madeira. "You know, Thomas, we must listen more carefully to Dr. Franklin, get him to speak up on more occasions—for he is a man who has lived in both a humble and a grand manner."

Jared leaned back and smiled, pouring himself a glass of Madeira. If only William could hear him now. He, Jared Mifflin, was actually making a difference, for William and for Henry. He felt he had earned himself some rest and relaxation for the remainder of the weekend.

CHAPTER TWELVE

JARED awoke on Monday ready and eager to get back to work; his mind raced as he thought of the days that lay ahead. The only thing the weekend had not resolved was the mystery of the letters. It didn't matter really, he thought, since Hetty clearly wasn't interested in the number of his letters, as she said, but what each one contained. What had him tossing and turning through the night, however, was that he had revealed detailed descriptions of the daily issues faced by the delegates. Suppose they had been intercepted— by a maid, or the butler, or even one of Hetty's brothers.

As he dressed, he wondered what trouble could be caused were his writings to land in any of these hands.

Anxious to stop on his way to work and see how Henry was, he momentarily put these thoughts aside and departed. A light summer rain had brought an end to the hot, sticky air of the weekend, making Jared's gait sprightly. The alleyway leading to the Indian Queen's stables was bustling with people departing on horseback. Jared assumed that Henry was feeling better when he saw him readying a carriage just outside the open doors of the stable. As he started toward his friend, a familiar voice called to him from across the street, taking Jared off his intended course.

"Master Mifflin, may we have a word?"

Jared turned and saw Nehemiah Weaver strutting toward him.

"I'm just on my way to work, Mr. Weaver," Jared said, trying to avoid a discussion. He started down Fourth Street and cut through Patton's Alley. "But if you care to accompany me," Jared offered, hoping he would decline, "perhaps we could talk along the way."

"I happen to be heading your way," Weaver said.

"I'll bet you were," Jared answered sarcastically.

The two were now walking side by side, Weaver working to match Jared's hurried pace.

"I know you are not at liberty to talk of the Convention as yet, master, but I thought perhaps you could give me a few nonpolitical observations about the weekend break. The public certainly could use a little human interest story or two."

"I've told you, Mr. Weaver," Jared said, feeling a bit exasperated, "that my thoughts and observations will remain my own."

"Oh, damn it, tell me something, will you? I've got a job to do. Of course, how should I expect the likes of you to understand what that means."

Jared stopped dead in his tracks.

"You privileged folk," Weaver continued, "couldn't possibly understand what it means to work for an honest wage. If I don't produce stories for the *Gazette*, I don't eat. Simple as that."

"Look," Jared said, "I'm not as I appear, Mr. Weaver, though I'm sure it's of no interest to you. You know, I've not always hailed from the so-called privileged class. As a matter of fact, I am beginning to understand your plight, at least where the Convention is concerned. But you must understand my position: When I take an oath, I stand by it. I swore to absolute secrecy, and I shall honor my word until I am released from it."

"But, Master Mifflin, this time I don't want political information . . . just a story or two about . . . the fox hunt out at the Bartram estate, for instance. Did the general lead the field?"

"I can't say," Jared answered. They were nearing the State House door as the clock in the tower chimed half after eight. "I really must go," Jared said.

"Wait, please," Weaver begged. "Just listen to me. I've been watching your movements, and I know you have friends at all levels. If you understand my problem, then you are probably also beginning to agree that the average citizen deserves to know what the delegates are up to. Furthermore, I am well aware that they are discussing the issue of slavery in regard to representation, and that the Convention is on the brink of disaster. That fact became obvious when Dr. Franklin called for daily prayer."

This last remark echoed in Jared's mind. How did Weaver know any of this? Especially his very own thoughts?

"How do you know what's happening?" Jared blurted out without thinking that he would be giving himself and the secrets of the Convention away.

"Ah, so it's true."

"I didn't say that," Jared protested.

"But you said enough for me to go on," Weaver retorted, quickly writing in his ever-present notebook.

"You can't quote me, Mr. Weaver," Jared protested. "I am only speaking from my own beliefs. These issues come from *Common Sense,* not from the Constitutional Convention," Jared lied, covering himself. "If you like, I will ask Mr. Madison today if there isn't some statement he could make for the press. But my lips are sealed," and with that he entered the State House.

He wound his way through several groups of delegates who were oddly early; he wondered if something special was finally going to occur.

"Good day, Dr. Franklin," he said as the old man hobbled into the chambers. *If he's just arrived,* Jared surmised, *that means William can't be far away.* His eyes darted to every corner of the East Room and the hallway until he spotted William drifting out the door.

"William, could I have a minute of your time?" Jared called, running to catch up with him. "I've got a problem and hope you can help."

"What is it?" William asked.

"That rascal reporter . . . you know the one . . . he's been hanging around here since the Convention began. I've seen him talking to you."

"You mean Weaver?" William queried. "What's he up to now?" he asked nonchalantly.

"Somehow he knows what's going on inside the East Room. Things I've told Hetty in my letters! I'm really worried, William, because I think someone in Hetty's household is reading my mail and talking to Weaver. That's the only thing I can come up with. I'm very concerned—if this continues, the leaks will surely be traced to me! Do you have any ideas?"

"I'll think about it. But offhand, I can't imagine how Weaver is getting anything."

Jared was thrown off by his friend's lack of a solution because William always had one. "Well, anyway, think about it, will you? Oh, and William, you have been giving my letters directly to Hetty, haven't you?"

"As a matter of fact, I haven't," William answered. His eyes were no longer meeting Jared's. "Half of the time she isn't home, so I leave them with the butler. Sometimes I simply place them by the door."

"But how could you—you know very well that what's at stake here is Hetty's reputation as well as the security of the Convention," Jared said, anxiety in his voice. "I would have paid you extra for the trouble if it meant going back a second time," he continued.

William was becoming edgy and clearly uncomfortable. "I don't want your extra money, Jared," William said. "A deal is a deal. Now I must go—I'm way off schedule."

Jared was dumbfounded by the whole situation. His conversation with William had further confused matters rather than shedding light on them. Wandering toward the main door, not wanting to take up his post just yet, he watched his friend saunter off down the center of the mall. Then William seemed to stop and turn toward some bushes as though someone was calling to him. Jared squinted, wondering who it could be as his friend walked out of view.

"Master Mifflin," Mr. Fry called from the corridor, "I'd be obliged if you could stand guard by the door for a moment."

Jared let the main door close gently and went back to his bench. He allowed himself to be swept up in the conversations behind the door.

"Gentlemen, gentlemen!" The voice of George Washington could be heard booming from the East Room. "Let us commence this session."

The hallway was clear for the moment, and Jared sat down on his bench with the intention of trying to piece together the happenings of the morning.

He was bothered by William's abrupt attitude at the end of their conversation. Hadn't he seen William chatting with Weaver on a number of occasions? Could it be that it was William betraying his trust . . . ? *Hetty insists that she isn't getting all the letters I've written—the count is almost twenty . . . William is the only person delivering them . . . Weaver makes mention of specific issues contained in the letters. . . . And today, William, for the first time ever, seems to have no advice and offered no assistance.*

Jared knew he had to have another talk with him. Although his cheeks burned at the thought of betrayal, he held on to the belief that William would never deliberately hurt him.

Despite his problems Jared was eager to hear what, if anything, would come to the floor as a result of his weekend discussions. The debates within the East Room were loud, and he was grateful for something else to think about.

"I request, nay, insist," he could hear General Pinckney protest, "that the productive peasants of the south be counted as whole men in this representation issue. After all," he continued, "we pay taxes for these slaves and support them in every other way. This is the least you can grant us."

"Never!" an irate voice shouted. "Never!" others chanted from various positions within the room.

Then Rufus King could be heard, shouting above the other raised voices. "I deplore counting slaves as whole persons in the issue of representation when they themselves are denied the vote and, in fact, any kind of liberty."

"Here, here!" others responded, tapping their canes in agreement. And then there was silence. So completely opposed were the two sides that Jared figured neither knew what to say next. At times like this, he always hoped that wise old Benjamin Franklin would pitch in. And as the standoff continued that was exactly what occurred.

"Gentlemen. May I have your attention!" Jared could hear a pin drop as the sage raised his voice. "We are sent here to consult, not to contend with each other.

"When a broad table is to be made and the edges of the planks do not fit, the artist takes a little from both and makes a good joint. In like manner here, both sides must part with some of their demands in order that they may join in some accommodating position."

Again silence. *Who would dare follow him?* Jared chuckled to himself.

Finally, Gunny Bedford asked for the floor. "With all due respect, sir," he said, "I do believe that if the large states continue their incessant push, the smaller ones will find themselves a foreign ally of greater honor and good faith who will take us by the hand and do us justice."

And so it went all afternoon. However, Jared sensed that at day's end most of the angry words had been spoken and were in the past. Somehow the delegates, as they left the East Room, seemed more relaxed, more resolved, and ready to return on the morrow to begin some sort of vote.

He was about to meet with Mr. Madison when he spotted William by the outside door. Their eyes met and William quickly turned away.

Jared decided that the time to confront the matter was at hand. "William," he called, approaching his friend.

"Yes, that's me," the other answered.

"I've a question to ask you. It's not an easy one, but I have no choice."

"I have no fear of your questions, Jared," William answered, his cocky spirit bright as ever.

"I'm beginning to believe that you aren't delivering all of my letters to Hetty. Could I be correct?"

William was speechless. After recovering a bit, he was able to inquire as to why Jared had such suspicions.

"Just a hunch," Jared said, studying William's face carefully.

William remained silent. Finally, he offered the feeble suggestion that several of the notes might have gotten lost when he was running his various chores.

"Master Ellsworth," old Mr. Fry said from the East Room doorway, "the doctor wishes to depart."

"Got to go, old chap," William said, slapping Jared's arm and racing down the hallway.

Frustrated and exasperated, Jared began his end-of-day chores. The next few days would bring him the necessary answers, and he hoped, deep in his heart, that William's guilt would not be confirmed.

There was an eerie silence in the East Room. The delegates were whispering, Jared guessed, or praying, or not speaking at all! To Jared it seemed like the calm before the storm, but he had stopped trying to guess the direction of the Convention. Besides, he had his own problems—William's apparent betrayal and no time off to see Hetty.

Just then he looked across at the now-crowded courtroom and spied William, in the far right corner, slightly hidden by a pillar, engaged in conversation. *Now what's he up to?* Jared found himself wondering, realizing the anger behind his thoughts.

Since their confrontation the week before, William had neatly avoided Jared, coming into the corridor only when it was full of delegates. Jared decided to approach William once again, but retreated when he noticed that his friend was in conversation with none other than Nehemiah Weaver. The two of them appeared to be bargaining . . . William holding up several fingers, Weaver shaking his head, William turning to go away, Weaver finally digging through his pockets and pulling into view a handful of bills.

Money! Jared said to himself, aghast. Weaver was now dealing bill after bill into William's outstretched hand, counting them out like playing cards. William handed him something, and Weaver slithered through the crowd, quietly making his way toward the exit. Tucked under his arm was a brown paper package.

Jared quit his hiding place and headed over to confront William.

"Making deals with members of the press, are you?" he inquired, startling William.

"It's none of your business, Mifflin," William responded abruptly.

"Why the nasty reaction?" Jared baited him. "Is that a bit of guilt?"

William began to back away, using the spectators as a sort of barricade between Jared and himself. "I have no reason to feel guilty," William stammered, now clearly trying to run away.

"Why have you been avoiding me?" Jared said through gritted teeth, the tone of his voice becoming uncontrollable.

"Order in the court!" the judge shouted from the courtroom, banging his gavel and attempting to turn the crowd's attention away from Jared.

With that, William turned, darted behind three portly peasants, and ran down the corridor.

Jared followed, nearly stumbling over two little children, and shoving aside a woman. With a burst of speed he was out the door and into the courtyard before the judge, the guards, or anyone else keeping order could detain him.

Already halfway across the State House Yard, William was heading for the south gate and was practically there. The only way for Jared to catch up was for him to plough through the neat plantings and well-placed shrubbery.

"You'll not get away with this!" Jared shouted as William turned and looked back at him. Losing his footing on the edge of a flower bed, William fell to his knees. Jared pounced, flipping him over onto his back and pinning his arms to the ground.

"How could you do this to me?" Jared screamed; he needed no further convincing. Jared's rage had built to a fever pitch during the chase. "Answer me!" he said, squeezing William's arms with brutish force. "You sold my letters, didn't you? Didn't you? Answer me! Say something, you scoundrel!"

William's struggle to release himself from Jared's grip was to no avail. "What do you want from me?" he shouted back, overtaken and overwhelmed.

"The truth, damn you—the truth for once, instead of your cock-and-bull stories."

William continued to writhe in an effort to escape from the weight of Jared's body. "If you would be so kind as to let me up," he grunted, "perhaps we could talk about this in a more civilized manner." His eyes focused on a group of spectators who had gathered around them.

Jared, now embarrassed at being so out of control, quickly let go and helped William to his feet.

"So what is it you want from me, Mifflin?" William asked, rising to a standing position and brushing off his breeches.

"A simple explanation! What did that brown package contain?"

William answered with a stare.

Jared continued to press, his voice now under control. "You did sell my letters, didn't you?"

"What if I did?" William countered, nonchalantly kicking a few pebbles as he strolled a few steps away from Jared.

"What if you did?" Jared asked incredulously, raising his voice again and grabbing William's arm. "You were my friend, and they were private!"

"Not so," William retorted. "They contained public information, if you want my opinion . . . information the citizens deserve to know," he went on. "What you may have perceived as something done with little forethought was something I agonized over. I was aware that in sharing your letters I was giving away privileged information. But after witnessing the true colors of those crusty old selfish delegates at Bartrams', it was an easy decision to rationalize. If I accomplish nothing else, I've made up my mind to give the average citizen in this so-called democracy of yours a chance to have some say in the laws that are about to be put into place. If you have a problem with that, too bloody bad! I have my conscience to live with; you have yours."

"Your rationalization is very interesting," Jared said, "but I trusted you, even paid you . . . we could have at least talked it through. I might even have agreed with your actions on some level. You know I've been reviewing my own thoughts and feelings in these past few weeks. You've chosen to judge me at face value and not look beyond my clothes and station."

"You may have had your eyes opened this last week or so, Jared, but you'll never understand what it is to always be thinking of your next move. I'm on my own, old chap, trying to find some sort of freedom. If I hope to survive, I have to pay my own way. Nothing will ever be handed to William Ellsworth. So I make a shilling wherever I can; if I earn it for a worthy cause, so much the better."

"Worthy cause? Exposing state secrets, compromising your friend's reputation, embarrassing Hetty Morris in the process . . . you call that worthy?" Not waiting for a response, Jared continued, "I've no more time to talk if I hope to fix this mess. Perhaps Hetty can help me put a stop to what you've started."

Without giving a thought to his responsibilities at the East Room, he sprinted across the yard, not sure where to head first. The clock struck three o'clock. He had but an hour to retrieve the letters and get back to Mr. Madison before the Convention adjourned.

Running toward Market Street, Jared chanted, "Please be home." He knew that if anyone could remedy this terrible situation, it was Hetty.

"Hetty!" he exclaimed, when she opened the door.

"Jared, you look awful. What's happened?"

"The worst possible thing. I need your help. Do you suppose you could get away?"

She looked back inside to make certain none of the servants were about. "Mother and the boys are out for the afternoon," she whispered. "If you can wait just a minute while I get my bonnet, I'll be right with you."

Jared leaned against the door frame to collect his breath. When she returned they walked quickly away from the house and turned onto Sixth Street.

"Now what is it?" she asked, taking hold of his arm.

"Do you remember how upset I was when we discussed my letters the night of the ball?"

She nodded.

"I've been afraid that perhaps they were being intercepted."

A look of uncertainty crossed her face.

"William Ellsworth hasn't been delivering all of my letters to you. He's been picking and choosing, and holding onto the rest. Well, he's just handed them over to Nehemiah Weaver, a reporter for the *Gazette*."

She gasped. "But why?"

"Because he saw they were full of political issues. He knew that the newspapers were ready to pay for any information about the Convention. We've got to get them back! If any secrets get into print, the entire Constitutional Convention could fall apart."

"What do you want me to do?" she asked, fully understanding the urgency of the situation.

"I'm hoping that the reporter in question did not go directly to the paper. He usually takes an early supper at the Indian Queen. If you could get over there, find Henry, and have him point the man out to you, perhaps you could charm the letters away from him. You're rather good at that, you know," Jared added, attempting to lighten their moods.

"What will you be doing?" she asked, trying not to call attention to the color rising in her cheeks.

"I can't leave my post any longer, Hetty, or I'll be in deeper trouble than I already am. I'll look for you the minute I get off work." He squeezed her hand and left. Hetty gathered up her flowing skirt and hurried down the street.

As Jared approached the State House, he was greeted by disturbing signs of mass confusion. Darting inside, he noticed that the East Room doors had been fully opened. Mr. Fry was pacing up and down at the far end of the corridor, and William Ellsworth was sitting in the center of the room surrounded by delegates.

"So, young man, what business did you have taking over the door?" Jona Dayton was asking. "Did you think you could actually get away with playing the part of Jared Mifflin? Everyone knows you're but a houseboy."

"It was not my intention to pass for Jared, sir. I was simply doing him a favor."

"A favor!" Uncle Thomas shouted. "By letting a maniac into these sacred chambers?"

"But, sir," William countered, "I didn't let him in. He simply got past Mr. Fry and me . . ."

Jared's heart sank. He couldn't quite grasp what had taken place in his absence, but clearly William was in the thick of it.

"We'll need some immediate answers, or it's the Walnut Street prison for you!" Jona Dayton said, pounding his fist.

Upon hearing that, Jared burst into the room and headed straight for the group.

"Jared," Mr. Madison said, sounding relieved. "Now we'll get to the bottom of this."

"Indeed," Gouverneur Morris chimed in. "One can never trust the riffraff. This young Englishman claims he's working for you, Jared? Would you kindly clarify things for us?"

"We're waiting for the truth," Uncle Thomas chimed in. "I'm confident that you would never be so foolish as to leave your responsibilities in the care of someone of his station."

"I beg your pardon, Uncle," Jared broke in, deeply upset by the rude characterization of William. Had this been Ebin or Jonathan, they would have been treated with *some* degree of dignity. "May I ask what is it that Master Ellsworth, who is, in fact, a trusted employee of Dr. Franklin's, has done to warrant such treatment?"

"He permitted an anti-Federalist rabble-rouser into these chambers, that's what," Uncle Thomas said indignantly. "He instigated the whole thing, for all we know," he continued. "As a result, look at the chaos. The Convention has been completely broken up—just at a time when we seemed to be nearing a compromise."

"Do you not think the blame should be directed at me, Uncle?" Jared suggested, moving into the circle and sitting next to the accused. "After all, William was not properly trained to do my job, and it was I who committed the crime of leaving my post in the first place."

As Jared stood his ground, he found it hard to believe that less than an hour before he had been fighting in the yard with William.

"Why *did* you leave, then?" Mr. Madison inquired, a calm tone in his voice. "I am certain, gentlemen, that Jared had good reason to do so. Would you care to tell us, Jared?" Mr. Madison asked.

Jared thought for a moment. "I'm sorry, sir," he answered. Swallowing slowly, he attempted to formulate a sensible answer. "I am not at liberty to discuss my reasons. I ask that you trust me. There are times when one must take actions to resolve existing situations without revealing what has transpired until afterward. I'm sure you can understand. After all, isn't that what the Convention is doing—making decisions in private and then sharing them with the public once the issues have been resolved?"

The men were speechless. Jared had spoken in their language, and they could say nothing in return.

"Well," Mr. Madison broke in, clearing his throat, "you've heard the young man. I think we've lost enough time with this rather minor ruckus, and I suggest that we call the delegates back into session."

Jared breathed a sigh of relief and turned toward William. "If you'll excuse us then," he said, jumping to his feet, "we shall both get back to our jobs. I can assure you that there will be no further incidents."

As Jared and William exited, the East Room doors closed behind them.

"Thanks, Jared," William said. "For a few minutes there, I thought it was all over for me. I'd best be off as I'm sure I should be packing my things. The doctor will certainly not keep me in his employ after he hears about this."

"Wait a minute, William. Quite frankly, after what has transpired today, 'thanks' just isn't enough," Jared said. "You can't take off without telling me what it was that went on in there."

"You looked so panicked when you ran off," William began, "that I decided to stay behind and watch the door to avoid any further complications. Almost immediately old man Fry wandered off, mumbling something about the heat. Then the water boy came to the back door to make his delivery. He needed help getting the barrel into the building, and when I left the bench to assist him someone stormed into the East Room; he must have been waiting for me to turn my back. It all happened so fast that I couldn't even tell you from whence he came."

"Who was he? What did he look like?" Jared asked, pushing for a description.

"No one got his name, but he was an elderly gentleman, very

well dressed. He began to read in a bold manner from something he called an anti-Federalist manifesto. He'd not read more than a sentence or two before several delegates and I approached him and led him from the chambers. He didn't even put up a fight. It was then that Mr. Madison looked around for you and, realizing that I was taking your place, led me into the East Room. I'm most apologetic, Jared, that my actions have caused you distress," William said, looking squarely into Jared's eyes. Jared was aware that he wasn't apologizing but simply expressing regret. "Perhaps," William continued, "there's still time to do something to protect your integrity."

"I'm afraid I'm at a loss to come up with a solution, William. Besides, I'm stuck here for the duration of this session. And the delegates have been meeting later and later each day."

"Let me see what I can do, all right?" William said, looking for a sign of approval.

Jared wasn't sure how to respond or whether he even wanted William's help. He said nothing as William took his leave, his once cocky walk all but gone. In its place was the gait of someone who was young and unsure of his path.

Alone with his thoughts, Jared could only hope that Hetty and Henry were having some success, because he was obviously stuck for a late afternoon session.

CHAPTER THIRTEEN

"PSST! Jared, come here!" the voice of Uncle Thomas whispered from a crack in the open East Room door.

Jared jumped up and obeyed, wondering what he could want. "Mr. Madison feels you should sit inside the door for the proceedings this afternoon."

"Inside?" Jared said. "But why?"

"He doesn't want any disturbances for the remainder of the day. There are many issues to be resolved, and you may be needed to carry messages or to meet the delegates' needs; if you are here, the men will not be compelled to leave the chamber."

"But Uncle, has my presence been approved?"

"Why, of course," he said, matter of factly; "Washington has already asked the members if they would object to your presence, and there was a resounding 'no.' Come, now, no more delays."

They entered quietly just as General Pinckney had taken the floor. Jared sat on a small stool beside the door.

A railing divided him from the delegates, and he couldn't help but think once again what an interesting cast of characters they made. He forgot the world outside the door for the time being. The East Room was much more untidy than he had expected—crumpled paper balls scattered about the floor, cluttered desk tops. He coughed several times, his throat feeling suddenly scratchy and dry because of the musty, hot air.

Mr. Madison seemed not to notice Jared's presence. He sat hunched over his ledgers, moving quill to inkwell and back to paper, only glancing up occasionally to record who was speaking. Mr. Madison had removed his jacket, as had many others. With the windows sealed shut the delegates were somewhat insulated from the stifling air during the morning. However, by afternoon the combination of stale, smoky air and tired bodies lent a pungent atmosphere to the prestigious proceedings.

General Pinckney was the most peculiar. Dressed elaborately, he possessed a pompous southern air that bordered on the effeminate.

"I ask you gentlemen once again," he began, "consider that we count our slaves as whole men. Surely this is one way to even up the population problems among the states."

Counting slaves as "whole men . . ." Jared thought, shaking his head and wincing at the manner in which the idea had been phrased. *What else are they if not whole?* Pinckney took a bit of snuff out of his box and brought it to his already upturned nose.

"Are you asking for a show of hands?" General Washington inquired.

Pinckney nodded.

"Well, then, all in favor say 'aye,' " the general said in a commanding voice. There were few.

"All opposed?" the general asked.

"Nay," resounded boldly throughout the room. Jared breathed a sigh of disappointment. *There seems to be little conscience on either side about the slave issue,* he thought.

Jared was pleased that Benjamin Franklin had arrived for the afternoon session. He had heard the doctor speak out on more than one occasion against slavery, and he had even formed a society that promoted the abolition of slavery. However, the doctor chose to remain silent.

Instead, Mr. Madison took the floor. *Finally,* Jared thought, *I get to see this man in action.* He couldn't quite imagine how the deep-thinking intellectual would fare as an orator. But according to Uncle Thomas, James Madison had spoken more than most of the delegates thus far.

"Gentlemen," he began in a stern, assertive tone, "I think the time has come to discuss the issue of proportional representation in both houses of Congress. We can delay no longer, as this question must be resolved before we can move on to the others. May I remind you once again that we are a body striving to create a union? We must leave behind the idea of state sovereignty and do away with petty state attachments that are a bone of contention to this country!"

Strongly put, Jared thought. *I'll wager we're in for some action now!*

Sure enough, bald-headed William Patterson barely waited for James Madison to sit down before jumping to his feet. "I must tell you, Mr. Madison, that I am here to fight for the community of New Jersey, which sent me to Philadelphia, and I will not, under any circumstances, forget my people. We—my colleagues and I—came to this Convention with a sound plan and intend to leave with a plan as acceptable to those citizens we so proudly serve as ours was."

"Here, here," craggy Roger Sherman mustered, his Yankee spirit getting the best of him. Jared sat on the edge of his chair, eager to hear what this elderly delegate had to say. Not only had he served in the Continental Congress, but he also had helped draft the Declaration of Independence. Now, even though his health was failing, he was determined, it seemed, to be a part of this major act. "I fear that anything short of equality of voice in one branch would mean an end to the state governments, gentlemen, and in time this could mean an end to the states themselves. This is something I am certain no man of sound mind would care to witness in this fine country of ours."

He sat down as quickly as he had risen, looking to his colleague, Dr. William Samuel Johnson, to finish their evidently collective thoughts. Jared had been intrigued by the other delegates' apparent respect for Johnson; they gathered almost nightly at the City Tavern to ask questions of him and to listen to his orations. Uncle Thomas had told Jared that of all the delegates, Johnson was certainly the most intellectual.

"America, my friends," Dr. Johnson began, "is now one political society composed of individuals. May I remind you that the states are political societies with individual interests and should remain as such? However, do not ignore the double-barreled nature of our society. The two houses of Congress are not opposed to each other. Rather they should be halves of a unique whole so that in one branch, the people themselves can be represented according to population; in the other, the states."

It sounds like a fair solution to me, Jared thought. He was moved by the serious and careful attention these men gave to their choice of language. The austere, upper-class, almost snobbish image the delegates presented outside the State House was practically non-existent inside this room. Sitting here, he could now better understand how important it was to keep these words and ideas quiet so they could put away their public airs and express their private feelings. How was it possible to clearly see both sides of the argument—William's and the delegates'?

Secrecy, Jared thought. The word was like a double-edged sword. *Would Hetty succeed in retrieving the letters, or was the information already being set into type at the* Gazette? *Who was right; was there a right or wrong?*

As the tension continued inside the East Room, Jared tried to forget his personal problems. James Madison rose to his feet. "Gentlemen," he began, "I must suggest to you once again that if the issue of representation can be adjusted, all other difficulties will be surmountable."

Mr. Madison's comment seemed to spur the others on. They continued long after their usual closing time. Jared chuckled as Uncle Thomas lit pipe after pipe, taking in the show but contributing little.

Funny, Jared thought, *he has an opinion on everything. Perhaps he's met his match in these delegates and can't find anything more to add.*

"Gentlemen, shall we put the matter to a vote?" John Dickenson said. Next to Thomas Paine's *Common Sense,* Jared respected Mr. Dickenson's book, *Letters from a Farmer,* more than any other. It also spoke about freedom and liberty for all. "I first put this matter of compromise before you on the second day of June. As it is now the sixteenth of July, I think it is time for a consensus to be reached. I therefore ask General Washington if we may vote on the plan that the lower house of the Congress reflect the population of each state by the number of representatives, and that the upper house be made up of equal representation from each state."

He sat down in the midst of a silent room. Jared gazed about at the men. Mr. Madison, head in hands, looked as though he was about to surrender a battle. Others seemed eager to get on with it.

The delegates huddled together, whispering among their respective state delegations, some stretching from one table to the next, others passing notes to members in front or behind them. Charles Pinckney approached Dr. Franklin and whispered in his ear. Jared watched the doctor maneuver his body around and wink at the rest of the South Carolina delegation.

Finally, General Washington rose from his seat and asked Secretary Jackson to read off the names of each state. "It is time for the vote," he inserted.

. . . "Connecticut: 'Aye.' Delaware: 'Aye.' New Jersey: 'Aye.' Pennsylvania: 'Nay.' South Carolina: 'Nay.' Virginia: 'Nay . . .' "

Jared kept a count on his fingers, noting the closeness of the vote: five in favor, four against, and one abstention.

Shock seized the room as the big states realized that they had been overruled. They quickly huddled around Mr. Madison to determine the next step. There followed a long discussion that Jared found amusing. One side had clearly emerged victorious, and yet these men continued the debate.

Mercifully, at half after six, General Washington moved to adjourn and to have a day of rest before commencing again. "I trust that by that time," he said, "you gentlemen will have resolved your differences on this matter and will feel ready to proceed to the other vital concerns that must be taken up by this group."

With that, the gavel hit the block and the delegates dispersed.

"Jared, my boy," Uncle Thomas said as he rambled out of the room, "you were witness to quite a day. What did you think?"

"I was waiting to hear what contribution you might make, Uncle. Did the cat get your tongue?" Jared joked. "I've never been seated in a room with you when you haven't had something to say."

"Now, don't jump to any conclusions about the contributions your old uncle does or does not make," he said as they moved toward the outside. "I do most of my work in the back rooms, if you know what I mean." With that came a mighty slap on Jared's back, and Uncle Thomas collapsed into an uncontrollable wave of laughter. "As a matter of fact," he continued once his flushed face returned to its natural pink color, "I will be attending a rather lengthy session tonight. As you know, Aunt Sarah and the girls are out in the country visiting the Roberts family. That gives you an evening to yourself. I can't imagine what you'll find to do!" he said, adding a wink to his comment.

"I could use a night to myself," Jared admitted, knowing that the letter controversy awaited him. "Where are you headed?"

"The Indian Queen—the large states must decide whether the close vote will make the compromise acceptable back home. We can't build a strong federal government on a series of compromises, you know. Have yourself a good evening," Uncle Thomas said with a smile, and then he quickly walked off after Mr. Fitzsimmons. "Oh, and Jared," he called back, "do give my best to Hetty Morris, won't you?" His laughter could be heard all the way down Chestnut Street.

Jared was famished. The Convention had never been in session this late. He had planned to take supper at the Indian Queen and to get some information from Henry, but in order to avoid the delegates, he'd have to make other plans. Surely Margaret would have something prepared; Uncle Thomas and Jared were expected home hours ago. He decided to stop for a quick supper before heading over to see Henry at the stable.

Walking down Market Street, he noticed a group of delegates knocking on Dr. Franklin's front door. He scooted up the side alleyway hoping to find William at the back of the house.

"William," Jared called out in a loud whisper. "Over here."

William plopped the punch bowl he was carrying onto the wicker table and ducked into Franklin's alley.

"Did you locate Henry or Hetty?" Jared asked anxiously.

"I waited by the Morris home for over an hour," William answered, "but there wasn't a sign of her. I had to leave and get back to work. As you can see, the doctor is having another gathering."

"Oh," Jared said. Disappointed and frustrated, he was able to think of no better response. "I was headed over to the Indian Queen until I discovered that my uncle and Mr. Madison were also taking dinner there. I suppose I'll slip over after dark. You best get back to work, William," Jared said, a tightness controlling his speech. Without another word, he turned and headed toward Chestnut Street.

"Surprise!" a female voice called.

"Hetty!" Jared exclaimed, as she popped out from behind the doctor's brick wall. "You scared me!"

"Little me, scare Jared Mifflin?" she teased. Grinning from ear to ear, she sashayed over to him.

"What are you doing out and about without an escort at this hour?" he asked. "'Tis not proper for a lady——"

"Shhh," she interrupted, putting her fingers to his lips. "When a young lady has business to attend to and her parents happen not to be in residence, she can and should do as she pleases. But where have *you* been?" she asked. "Henry and I have been past the State House a hundred times and you were not to be found."

"Of all days, this afternoon I was asked to sit inside the chambers. But that's another story. Were you able to retrieve the package?"

"Now, now, Jared, I don't think we should discuss this matter out here on the street."

"Well, where do you propose we go?" he asked, wondering what she was up to.

Just then she dashed behind the wall and produced a large basket filled with a variety of delicious-looking foods. "I think we should head for our spot by the river. There's still some daylight left, and I'm in the mood for a celebration tonight!"

"Then you succeeded! Oh, Hetty, I knew you would!" Jared exclaimed, scooping her up into his arms and twirling her around on the footway.

"Put me down," she wailed in mock concern. "Jared; people will see!"

"I don't care," he answered. A piece of fruit bounced into the street, and the two of them laughed. "I'm of a mind to give you a big kiss right here," Jared said, gently letting her down.

"Don't you dare. But do let us proceed to the riverbank," she said saucily, motioning for him to follow as she ran across the broad concourse.

It was a cloudy, cool evening, and the streets were fairly empty. Hetty took Jared's arm as they walked toward the Schuylkill River.

"Well, where are they?" he asked.

"What?" she said mischievously.

"The letters, silly. Do you really have them?"

"Right here," she answered, patting the bottom of her picnic basket.

"Let me carry that for you," Jared said, attempting to steal it from her firm grip.

"Oh, no you don't," she teased. "You'll see them soon enough."

"At least tell me what happened—and start from the beginning," Jared said, unable to wait another moment.

"I must say, Henry was wonderful!" Hetty began. "I went straight to the Indian Queen, and explained the problem to him. He was eager to help. Anyway, there was another livery boy on duty so he was able to immediately step away. We went to the front of the tavern so we could peer through the windows."

They were nearing the riverbank now. "Let's sit over there on the knoll, Hetty," Jared suggested. "We'll have a pleasant breeze as well as a beautiful view."

Jared found a level spot and removed his jacket so Hetty's pale blue dress would not be soiled. He arranged himself on his waistcoat, undoing his ruffled collar and feeling relaxed for the first time all day.

"All right now, we're settled," Jared said. "Go on."

"Well, we tried to spot Mr. Weaver through the stained-glass windows, but it was hopeless." She continued the story as she spread out cold chicken, fresh muffins, meat pies, fruit, and even lemonade on the cloth she brought. "As I had no idea what the man looks like, I stood by helpless. However, I *was* trying to figure out our next move, in the event that Mr. Weaver was not in the tavern."

"Well, was he?" Jared asked anxiously.

"Henry finally saw him. At least he was fairly sure he had. He told me to stay by the front door while he went around through the servants' entrance and peeked into the tavern. Within minutes he was back. Not only was Weaver still taking his meal, but sitting on the chair beside him was the package."

" 'Now, what do you suppose we should do?' I asked him. What I hadn't figured out was what our next move should be if Mr. Weaver *was* inside. So we sat down to think on a bench across the street. Henry said that if he was caught stealing, any future he hoped to have here or in Georgia would be dashed."

"What did you come up with?" Jared probed. "C'mon, Hetty, tell me."

"Would you care for some lemonade?" she asked, dragging out the scene and enjoying Jared's impatience.

"Sure. Fine," Jared said, exasperated but at the same time seeing the humor of the situation.

"Well, I knew that ladies, with the exception of barmaids—of which I am obviously not one—are not welcome anywhere near a tavern. So I asked Henry what he supposed would happen if I actually entered the tavern room, walked right up to Mr. Thompson, and asked him a question."

"You didn't!" Jared said, aghast that Hetty would even entertain such an idea.

"Henry said the whole tavern would be in chaos. The only time he remembered a woman on the premises, she was looking for her husband. The patrons either were in a state of shock or loudly registered a protest with Mr. Thompson."

Jared knew what was coming. Hetty's spunky attitude was perfect for just such a scandalous scene.

Hetty went on. "When I heard Henry's story, I knew we had a plan. Henry went into the kitchen and put on a waiter's cloak. When he appeared in the kitchen doorway with tray in hand, I walked into the tavern, pretending to be in search of my father. I headed for the bar where Mr. Thompson was standing—his mouth dropped open at my approach. At first the room was deathly quiet. Then all sorts of protests and confusion began. That's when Henry entered with a tray full of food, and while all eyes were on me he slipped by Nehemiah Weaver's table, picked up the package, and hid it under the tray until he was out of the room."

"Bravo!" Jared cheered.

"And Jared," she said, digging into the picnic basket, "here are the goods!" He reached for them.

"Now, just you wait," she said, placing the package in her lap and carefully untying the string. "I want to see if you really did write to me as often as you claimed. For all I know the package contains a journal or perhaps even letters to other young ladies.

"Hmmm," she said, leafing methodically through the stack. "Why, Jared Mifflin. I do declare, I think you have taken a fancy to me. Seven, eight, nine, ten, fifteen, there must be twenty letters in all! Do I still get to read them, even though they do contain state secrets?"

He smiled, feeling so many emotions—relief, happiness, contentment. Without a word he moved onto his knees. Leaning over, he took Hetty's cheeks in his hands and kissed her. They remained—with unread letters and half-eaten food around them—until darkness descended.

CHAPTER FOURTEEN

JARED had been waiting for over an hour while Mr. Claypoole and his men worked feverishly to finish the printing of the first draft of the Constitution. He watched as the apprentice pounded the ink beaters across each sheet of parchment, clamping the press atop it and sliding it through the great wooden printing machine. He could barely control his desire to read the copies that were drying on the ledge behind the railing that separated him from the men. But he dared not even move in that direction. The shop was charged with a sense of urgency as workers rushed to finish the job that had come as a direct order from General Washington.

A young boy stood by the front door to keep a line of waiting patrons from entering the shop. Mr. Claypoole seemed to want no distraction while his tall, slender frame was bent over the government papers spread before him. His print shop had prepared the documents for the Continental Congress and he was accustomed to such pressures. Jared could see by his tight-lipped expression that Mr. Claypoole was well aware of the importance of this document.

"Master Mifflin," he said, "we shall be finished shortly."

"Thank you, sir," Jared said, walking over to the railing. His heart skipped a beat when he realized that he would be one of the first to actually handle the Constitution.

"We're running off a few extra copies," Mr. Claypoole explained, wiping his ink-stained hands across his dark brown leather apron, "because the first few are a bit smudged."

He picked up a clean sample and brought it over to Jared.

"What do you think of the layout?" he asked proudly.

Jared scanned the seven sheets, more eager to read the content than comment on its format. "It looks quite good, sir," he managed, "although I must ask why it is so lopsided."

"So that they can make notes in the margins," Mr. Claypoole explained. "Those men over at the State House will be making plenty of changes before we print a final draft. That's why we've only printed sixty copies."

"I see," Jared said weakly. He had been under the impression that the completion of this first draft meant that final agreement had been reached.

It was already the sixth of August, and Jared had hoped for *some* free time before leaving for Princeton. *Perhaps Mr. Claypoole is wrong,* Jared thought hopefully. *After all, he hasn't been sitting outside the East Room door all summer, and he hasn't been privy to Uncle Thomas's after-hour conversations.*

"Here you go," Mr. Claypoole said, struggling to lift the heavy package over the railing. He had rolled up the precious copies and wrapped them in brown paper. "You best scoot over to the State House, master. I daresay this country cannot wait much longer for its Constitution."

"Thank you, sir," Jared answered, tipping his black felt hat to the young man who opened the door for him. He hurried down Second Street to Chestnut and was out of breath by the time he covered the four blocks to the State House.

Mr. Madison didn't see or hear him approach, so busy was he taking notes. Jared leaned down and whispered, "Sir, here are the copies." He carefully untied the string and placed the bundle in front of Mr. Madison. "I think it looks wonderful."

Mr. Madison skimmed the first paragraph and winked. "It looks good, my boy," he said. "A few more weeks and it will be all over."

A few more weeks! Jared thought as he left the room. *What more can they write?*

The corridor was stuffier than usual. He wanted to loosen his collar and remove his jacket, but he knew that would be improper. The dull green walls seemed duller and greener today, and he felt as though the three pillars that he had learned to live with all summer were about to tumble upon him. Craving a cool drink, he wiped his perspiring brow and tried to imagine himself sipping a chilled glass of lemonade.

"Wilting in the heat?" a female voice asked, just as he had closed his eyes and leaned his head against the wall.

"Hetty! What a pleasant surprise to see a lady inside the grand hall."

"I must admit I'm getting accustomed to wandering into places where ladies aren't supposed to," she joked, taking a few steps about the area, eyeing Mr. Fry, and gazing up and down at the East Room door as though she was surveying the scene for a sketch. "So this is where you've spent most of your summer," she teased.

"This is the place . . . here and inside with Mr. Madison. I must admit that until right now the setting has been terribly dull." Jared gave Hetty a devilish smile. He couldn't tell whether her smooth complexion was flushed from the heat or if he had again given her reason to blush. "Tell me, what brings you here?" he asked. Though Hetty had been sketching in the Yard all summer, this marked her first visit inside.

"I just stopped by to see you," she answered coyly. "I didn't want the Convention to end before I observed Jared Mifflin at work. Perhaps I should take a seat across from you and prepare to sketch the scene when the doors open."

"You should take the idea seriously, Hetty," Jared said, "and try to do so soon. Do you know that I delivered the first draft of the Constitution today?"

"You did!" she said. "You mean the Convention's almost over?"

*The East Room entry and interior hall, as seen
from the archway leading to the bell tower*

"Mr. Madison said it should only be a few more weeks," Jared said. The prospect of spending some of the remaining time practically working alongside Hetty made his seemingly never-ending summer job fresh with promise. "If you were sketching, we would be able to spend time together even if I can't manage the spare time we've both been hoping for."

Just then Mr. Fry coughed and Hetty was made aware that he was staring at her. "I must confess, however, that my visit is not without a purpose," she said loud enough for Mr. Fry to hear. She pulled a note out of her bag. "Mother asked me to deliver this note to Father when the session is over. She says it's quite important. Could you see that he gets it, Jared?" She winked and handed over the note. Jared glanced down, noticing that it was a blank piece of paper. *Why, Hetty Morris,* he thought to himself, *you'd think by now I'd know what to expect from you. You'd never simply walk in and pass up an opportunity to turn things upside down.*

"Certainly," he said, happy to be putting Mr. Fry in his place. "But do come back. I think it most important that you sketch the interior of these halls."

Turning on her heels, she was off, her pale green skirt swishing from side to side as she exited.

". . . therefore, gentlemen . . ." James Wilson was saying. Jared leaned back against the wall and listened. "I'm of the opinion that we should adjourn for the remainder of the day," he continued, "to permit each of us time to study the document and make our individual adjustments. I move that we resume on the morrow with our suggestions and additions."

"Here, here," the others echoed unanimously. The pounding gavel officially closed the day's session.

Jared had never seen the room empty so quickly. Only James Madison stayed behind.

"You're not running off to your chambers?" Jared asked after the other delegates had departed. "You must be just as anxious as the others to study the document."

"By now, Jared, I've practically memorized it. The Committee of Detail has been sharing their thoughts with me nightly." He leaned back in his chair and removed his glasses, pressing his fingers to his eyelids, a gesture that was disturbingly familiar to Jared. Mr. Madison did this only when he was drained or concerned.

"It seems to me, sir, that you should be breathing a sigh of relief," Jared said as he gathered up papers and notes left behind on the floor.

"If only you knew how many issues still need to be settled, Jared," Mr. Madison sighed. "There remains great debate over how to handle the slavery issue, as well as many other details in language and style. Why, we haven't even settled on how to elect the president of our country. I suppose tomorrow will tell how much fight is left in everyone. One thing is certain: We can count on Charles Pinckney and Alexander Hamilton to want several changes. As for the others . . . it is important that each one leaves Philadelphia feeling satisfied that he's left a mark on the Constitution. That way they'll have the will and stamina to work hard for ratification back home in their individual states."

"I see," Jared remarked. He was trying not to spill ink as he filled up the wells. "I must confess that I never thought much about what is to happen after Philadelphia."

"This is a democracy, Jared, and the Constitution must be acceptable to everyone. When we complete our task here, I can only hope that this document will reflect the sentiments and wishes of all thirteen colonies."

"Then all my worries about fifty-five men deciding the fate of our country have been in vain?"

"Indeed, my boy," Mr. Madison said with a smile. "After our work is finished, this document must be approved by hundreds, perhaps thousands of people. Every state legislature will read it, as will all interested citizens. As soon as we have a final draft, the newspapers are free to print it as they wish."

The daily sessions dragged on—Mr. Madison's predictions held strong. Clause after clause was debated. There were twenty-three articles to go through, and each one was picked over, if not for content, then for style. In the three weeks that followed, some provisions were dropped, others added, and much of the debate centered around refining the language. Every delegate needed to take home a paper that contained language which his state would find familiar and suitable.

Jared began to keep a record now that secrecy was less of an issue. He had come to understand why certain delegates fought so hard for specific points. For instance, Oliver Ellsworth, who had served long and hard in the old Congress raising money to pay off the war debt, pushed through the federal government's authority to impose and collect taxes. And Rufus King, who traveled extensively between the two great shipping ports of New York and Boston, cared about the regulation of trade. Alexander Hamilton, who had returned to play a part in the final discussions, insisted that an organized army was a necessary evil in this new country, for protection against the Indians as well as further intrusion from the British and Spanish. James Wilson cared deeply that promising citizens not be excluded from holding public office simply because they were new to the country. As a Scottish immigrant, he knew such prejudice personally.

Mr. Wilson could be heard daily explaining and answering questions on almost every issue. Like James Madison he had practically memorized the draft. Jared felt sure he would continue to guide the delegates through to the end, much like the good captain of a mighty ship.

Snobbish Charles Pinckney argued that senators and congressmen must own a certain amount of property to be elected. Fortunately, Benjamin Franklin reasoned that in so doing the spirit of the common man would be broken. And so, the delegates voted with Dr. Franklin, therefore making it possible for a man to run on ability rather than wealth.

Jared couldn't believe it when a Virginia delegate, George Mason, objected to slavery on moral grounds, siding with many of the northerners. At one point it seemed that the Convention was again at a standstill until someone had the sense to form a special committee that would make recommendations to the whole. In the end John Rutledge got his way on the slavery issue. It was decided that Congress could make no laws prohibiting the import of slaves and no ruling on slavery for another twenty years.

Jared could not understand how these men, seeking liberty and justice for all, could ride the fence in the case of the Negroes. True, he reasoned, the nation needed all the workers it could employ to build up a strong economy, but must Negroes be denied liberty in the process? Why must the Negro wait twenty years for a free life? Wouldn't they be just as productive on their own? Jared found himself wishing he were twenty years older so his thoughts could have the impact he so yearned for.

The weeks ran together—with Hetty making daily visits to the Yard and the Convention coming to a dramatic climax, Jared no longer counted days. Between the headiness of his courtship and his constant note-taking, he hadn't really noticed that William Ellsworth had all but disappeared. Dr. Franklin was being delivered each day by four prisoners from the Walnut Street jail with no assistance from William.

"May I be of help, Doctor?" Jared asked Benjamin Franklin as he moved slowly down the hall one afternoon.

"I'd be obliged, young man. Now that my houseboy is involved in other activities, I'm happy to accept your offer."

"I've been meaning to inquire as to his whereabouts, sir."

"I'm not sure what's on that lad's mind," the doctor said, shaking his head with confusion. "A few weeks back he asked for a change of duty . . . felt he could be of greater service in and around the confines of my home. I must say he is inexhaustible; he works night and day. He's even taken to repairing some of my machines. Handy fellow, William is."

That certainly doesn't sound like William, Jared thought. Something was amiss. He guided the weakened doctor into the sedan chair, closed the door, and waved him off.

What could Ellsworth be up to? Jared wondered as he went back into the State House. The William he had come to know was only content when he was in the thick of things, free to move about, connecting with sailors and servants and vendors.

Jared hastily finished up and went straight to Dr. Franklin's house, entering by way of the servants' entrance. He found William repairing a wagon wheel.

"Jared!" he said, looking mildly surprised, but happy to see his old friend. "I wasn't sure I'd see you again. . . . If you want to know the truth, I wasn't sure you wanted to see me."

"Well, you're the one who's been hiding," Jared answered. "I figured you weren't coming to the State House because of the ruckus we caused——" they both laughed.

"Well, that was partly my reasoning. But moreover, I've actually been *hiding*. Nehemiah Weaver's after me."

"Weaver! I thought we'd seen the last of him. What does he want?"

"It's my guess that he wants his money back. He's hanging around this house night and day—I'm virtually a prisoner. If I continue to please the doctor—and he's given me a raise, you know— with the money I received for selling the letters and my extra wages, I'll be able to leave Philadelphia within the next couple of weeks. I want to get back to my uncle, Jared."

"You mean you never gave him back the money?"

"Why should I have?" William asked, cocky as ever.

"William, he never got the information he wanted. I'm sure you know that," Jared countered.

"I still don't know what happened," William said. "What I do know is that I comb Dr. Franklin's *Gazette* every day, and there's been nothing about the Convention as yet. He probably thinks *I* swindled him.''

"Well, didn't you, really, when you think about it?''

"No matter how you look at it, that man is after my hide. Do you have any suggestions, Jared?''.

Jared was surprised at the question. He had known William all summer long, and not once had he needed advice.

"William, you probably won't like my suggestions.''

"Go ahead,'' William said. "Try me. I'm getting fairly desperate.''

"You know how I feel about honor,'' Jared began, trying hard not to sound like his uncle. "With the Convention continuing on for a few more weeks at least, it seems awfully stupid for you to be living like a monk.''

"It's not so bad, really,'' William said. "Dr. Franklin has given me a few drafting jobs . . . inventions he had in progress before the summer. I'm also organizing a file detailing everything he has ever created: works in progress, and would you believe it, ideas he has for the future! He needs another lifetime to finish all the work he has planned.''

Jared was half listening as he continued to come up with some sort of solution for his friend.

"I think you should give the money back,'' he interrupted.

"You must be kidding,'' William answered. "That's your idea of a solution? I need every shilling I have to get my uncle out of prison.''

"I know that,'' Jared said, preparing to counter any of William's objections. "But you want to leave town honorably, don't you? Besides, you've made such an impression on Dr. Franklin that it would be a shame to jeopardize that. Think about it. The scene in the East Room is behind you, and Dr. Franklin thought it more funny than anything else. But suppose Weaver gets desperate enough to blackmail you? He makes no bones about how hard he works. Suppose he goes to the doctor and tells him what you did . . . selling the letters, giving away Convention secrets . . . do you want that to happen?

"Listen," Jared continued, his mind racing with alternatives, "I've just learned that Mr. Madison will be needing couriers to distribute copies of the Constitution to the colonies. If I could get you such a position, you would not only get a horse, but a salary, *and* a way back to Massachusetts. What do you think? Would that be enough of an incentive to return the money?"

"Depends on how much," William answered.

"I'll ask my uncle tonight, and I should have an answer for you in the morning." He got up to leave.

"Tell me, before you leave, how's everything going with Hetty?" William asked. He seemed to be grappling for conversation so that their meeting would not end.

"Fine, really fine. She and Henry retrieved the letters, by the way. They cooked up a terribly clever scheme. I'll tell you all about it when I come by again."

"I'll look forward to that," William said. "Well, I best be off to the kitchen. I have almost no spare time these days. Thanks for stopping by, Jared," he said, walking toward the house without looking back.

Jared wished there wasn't a strain between them. William turned at the back door. "Oh, I forgot to ask you about Henry. What are his plans?"

"He's going back to Georgia," Jared said. "See you tomorrow." He meandered down Dr. Franklin's alley with a melancholy air overpowering him. He hadn't realized how attached he'd gotten to William and Henry. Despite their differences, his eyes had been opened by both of them. It was sad that the summer had to end.

Jared wandered about the town late into the evening. By the time he dragged himself home and crawled into bed, the lamplighter had long since brightened the streets.

CHAPTER FIFTEEN

WE, the People of the United States, in order to form a more perfect Union, Establish Justice, insure domestic Tranquillity, provide for the common defense, promote the general Welfare, and secure the Blessings of Liberty to ourselves and our Posterity, do ordain and establish this Constitution for the United States of America . . .

As Secretary Jackson continued to read, Jared stood in the back of the East Room gazing upon the delegates, none of whom moved a hair as they listened to the words they had labored so hard to formulate into a sturdy document. *Another hour or so, and the whole thing will be over,* Jared thought, a tinge of sadness stirring his soul as he realized his unique experience was coming to an end.

The windows of the East Room had finally been opened, allowing an unfamiliar cool breeze to descend upon the delegates at this, their last official meeting.

Jared could hear the stirrings of the crowd now gathering outside. He could picture Nehemiah Weaver, who probably had his ear pressed against the window's ledge in order to be the first to copy down the important words. William also would be among the crowd, packed and ready to depart, he supposed, the moment he was given copies of the Constitution to deliver. Jared wondered if Hetty was about, ready as ever to capture the departure scene on her sketch pad. Henry had given notice at the Indian Queen a week ago in order to spend his last week of "freedom," as he put it, drinking up city life before returning to Abraham Baldwin's plantation.

"And so, let it be Done," General Jackson began the final phrase that now was familiar to Jared because he had read and reread Uncle Thomas's first draft, ". . . in convention by the unanimous consent of the states present, the seventeenth day of September in the year of our Lord, One Thousand Seven Hundred and Eighty Seven and of the Independence of the United States of America the Twelfth. In witness whereof we have hereunto subscribed our names."

Jared gazed about the room, wondering what would happen next. He focused on General Washington, assuming that he would make the next move. There were some stirrings from the Virginians. *They're probably thinking up last-minute suggestions,* Jared surmised. Suddenly, George Mason asked for the floor. Everyone was sitting on the edge of their chairs.

"Gentlemen," he said in a strong, bold tone, "after much soul-searching I must inform you that since this Constitution does not yet contain a Bill of Rights I cannot, in all good conscience, subscribe to the document that lays waiting."

Jared was stunned. Mr. Mason's attendance during the summer had been almost perfect, and he'd sat on many committees. How could he not sign? No sooner had he taken his seat than Virginia's Governor Randolph rose—to agree with George Mason. "I will gladly present this Constitution to the legislature in Virginia but cannot, at this time, find it in my heart to put name to paper."

Now the room was full of rumblings. Governor Randolph had been one of the early arrivals and the first to speak at the opening of the Convention. He was the one who presented the Virginia Plan, Jared recalled—the paper on which the new Constitution drew some of its ideas! The various states were now huddled together in discussion and General Washington had to bang the gavel several times to bring order to the room. *How many others would follow suit?* Jared wondered.

"I must inform my colleagues that I, too, will not sign this Constitution in its present form," Elbridge Gerry of Massachusetts announced from his seat at the back of the room.

Here we go, Jared thought. *Divisiveness spreading once again from state to state.*

"Mr. President," the voice of Alexander Hamilton rose from the other side of the room. "May I speak?"

Washington nodded, not a trace of emotion on his stoic face.

Jared turned to look at Mr. Hamilton, the man responsible for calling the meeting at Annapolis, where the writing of a Constitution was first discussed. More than anyone else, it seemed that Alexander Hamilton cared about nationhood. He had written numerous articles and papers advocating a strong federal government. Ironically he'd had to endure a delegation that completely disagreed with him throughout this Convention.

"I must express my deepest anxiety that every member should sign," he said with an urgency in his voice. "If a few characters of consequence refuse to sign, their actions could do infinite mischief by kindling latent sparks which lurk under the general enthusiasm for this Constitution." He sat down, but did not take his eyes off Governor Randolph, to whom he was obviously delivering these brief but firmly stated remarks.

There was momentary silence. Jared wished that General Washington would rise and simply commence the signing. Instead, yet another delegate took the floor. *Oh, no*, Jared thought, *another Massachusetts man. Will he also dissent?*

Nathaniel Gorham instead moved that the stipulation for representation in the House be changed from one representative per forty thousand citizens to one per thirty thousand. *How could they change anything now?* Jared wondered, as he gazed over at the beautifully printed pieces of parchment that were spread out on the table. *With this latest diversion, the Convention will surely trail on for days*, he sighed. Knowing how meticulously these men had worked over this document, clause by clause, article by article, Jared resigned himself to the delay and took a seat on the stool provided for him by the door.

Rufus King seconded the motion, and Jared got set to watch yet another debate on representation. But instead, General Washington rose from his seat to make a statement. "Being the presiding member," he informed the group, "I know I am not at liberty to comment one way or another and have not done so until this moment. However, I must agree with my colleagues," he continued. "It has always appeared to me that an exceptional plan would be to have one representative for every thirty thousand citizens, and it would give me much satisfaction to see it adopted."

That did it. Everyone agreed to vote with the man considered to be the foremost of all Americans. With the representation issue finally put to rest and no one else jumping up with final objections, Dr. Franklin asked for the floor.

Finally! Jared said to himself. *Not many men here are going to disagree with Benjamin Franklin, no matter what he says.*

"Due to a weakened voice, gentlemen," he began, "I have asked my friend James Wilson to read you my sentiments on this momentous day." He nodded for Wilson to begin:

"Mr. President, I confess that there are several parts of this Constitution which I do not at present approve, but I am not sure I shall ever approve them. For having lived a long time, I have experienced many instances of being obliged by better information or fuller consideration to change opinions even on important subjects which I once thought right, but found to be otherwise.

It is, therefore, that the older I grow, the more apt I am to doubt my own judgment, and to pay more respect to the judgment of others.

In these sentiments, sir, I agree to this Constitution with

all its faults, if they are such. . . . I doubt, too, whether any other convention we can obtain, may be able to make a better Constitution.

For when you assemble a number of men to have the advantage of their joint wisdom, you inevitably assemble with those men all their prejudices, their passions, their errors of opinion, their local interest, and their selfish views. From such an assembly can a perfect production be expected?

It, therefore, astonishes me, sir, to find this system approaching so near to perfection as it does; and I think it will astonish our enemies. . . .

Thus I consent, sir. I cannot help expressing a wish that every member of the Convention who may still have objections to it, would with me, on this occasion, doubt a little of his own infallibility, and to make manifest our unanimity, put his name to this instrument."

Good old Dr. Franklin! Jared felt like running down the center aisle and giving the man a pat on the back. *No one will dare raise another issue,* he thought, and he was right. General Washington rose almost on cue to suggest that the signing commence.

Jared could hear a pin drop as George Washington stepped slowly off the balcony, where he had been perched for the last one hundred days, and strode toward the table upon which the Constitution lay. "Every king looks like a valet next to Washington," Jared recalled someone saying, *and whoever had said it was right!* he thought as he watched the general cross the room.

The five magnificently printed pieces of parchment had been laid out in a perfect row, their cream color glowing as they rested on the green baize that covered the tabletop.

Shining brightly in the center of the table and casting an occasional reflection about the room was Philip Syng's pen and ink holder. Probably the finest silversmith in all of the thirteen colonies, Mr. Syng had designed the set especially for the signing of the Declaration of Independence. Now, once again, his beautiful piece of craftsmanship would be used to help cement the fate of the new nation.

Jared could hear the scratchy sound of quill sliding across paper as General Washington signed his name.

His signature affixed, the general returned to his seat. *He must feel relief,* Jared thought. *He's been imploring these men to do* something *to create a stronger government for years.*

Thereafter, each state delegation followed suit. A feeling of utter peace descended on the East Room. Yet, Jared noticed, there seemed to be a sense of sadness registering on many of the faces. Most turned and nodded at Benjamin Franklin before walking back to their respective seats. Perhaps many of the delegates knew they would never again serve with this beloved citizen. Jared also thought that perhaps many realized that this particular group would never again have an opportunity to work together—at least not with the same intensity and certainly not for a cause as worthy as this one.

Over the past one hundred days, Jared had gotten to know these men. He was well aware how important the nation was to each of them. Some had fought in the Revolution, others helped draw up the Articles of Confederation, and still others sat on the Continental Congress. Tom Paine's words came flashing through Jared's head as he watched each man take his turn signing the document: "Those who expect to reap the blessings of freedom must undergo the fatigue of supporting them."

As the powder was sprinkled over the thirty-ninth signature, the clock struck four o'clock. General Washington exited first as usual, and by the time he reached the Chestnut Street doorway the roar of the crowd had become deafening. It was done.

"Mr. Madison," Jared said, racing down the aisle. He could stay silent no longer. "Congratulations!" he called, interrupting several other well-wishers.

"We did it, my boy, we did it!" Mr. Madison exclaimed with uncharacteristic enthusiasm, clasping Jared's arms as the two shook hands.

"I beg your pardon," Jared said, "but I believe that it is *you*, sir, who did it."

"With your help and the help of those around me. It has been a long summer, Jared, but one I feel this nation shall never forget. And as for you, my boy, I plan to see quite a bit of you in the future, perhaps in our new Congress . . . yes?" he questioned.

"It would be my honor, sir," Jared responded.

"Well, here you go, Jared," Mr. Madison said, lifting the heavy pile of documents that lay on his desk and handing them to Jared. "You know where they must go. It's up to the people now," he said. Jared walked slowly up the aisle. *In my arms I carry the future*, he thought as he reached the familiar East Room doors.

He stopped briefly for one last look, and as he turned to leave bumped straight into William Ellsworth.

"What have you been doing?" William asked. "My horse is getting restless, and so am I for that matter. I want to be the first courier to reach New England, Jared. Hand them over," he said, reaching out for his copies of the Constitution.

"Now, just you wait a minute," Jared answered back, taking one copy off the top of the pile. "Wouldn't you like the pleasure of giving this one to Nehemiah Weaver? He's been hanging around here since early this morning."

"I'd be delighted," William answered, grabbing the paper and darting out of the building.

"And when you're finished," Jared shouted, "some of us want to say a proper good-bye, do you hear!"

Jared leaned against the corridor wall to get his bearings. It was good to see the old William emerge again.

"Come on, Jared," he heard Uncle Thomas say. "We've been here long enough, don't you think?" Pulling Jared from the wall, he gave his nephew a customary slap on the back. "I've got to come back here tomorrow and read the thing to the Pennsylvania legislature. Can you believe that?"

"Sorry I won't be here to listen, Uncle," Jared answered, honestly

As the delegates depart, the Constitutional Convention
comes to an end.

feeling regret. "I'm already two days late for university, you know, and for a few uncertain moments today, I thought I'd be even later. I'd say that was a pretty close call—the signing, I mean."

"We knew there would be a few who held back. The way I look at it, it's their loss. It's a good Constitution, my boy, wouldn't you agree?"

Jared nodded as they walked into the bright sunlight. He spotted Hetty and Henry almost immediately. They stood apart from the expectant crowd in the southwest corner.

"Excuse me, Uncle. I have some business to attend to." He bolted through the groups of amassed people just as William was about to mount his horse. "Oh, no you don't," Jared said, grabbing William's arm and dragging him along to see Hetty and Henry.

"Well, it's over. I listened as best I could through the window," Hetty said, pointing to the only window under which there was a stump to stand upon. "By the way, I didn't hear one thing mentioned about the ladies. Did they or did they not talk about the fairer sex in our new Constitution?"

Jared hated to answer her. "I'm afraid I heard nothing," he admitted.

"I thought as much," she replied, a tone of resignation in her voice. "Well, I suppose it gives us something to work for."

"And work you will," William chimed in. "I've met few people with your determination. Jared, I would say you have yourself a mighty strong lady here. You'd best hold on to her—if you can, that is!"

Everyone laughed, including Hetty.

"And Henry, before you even ask," Jared said, "I'm ashamed to say that the delegates devoted only a few lines to the issue of slavery. You opened my eyes to a lot of injustices. All I can say is that if I ever make it to Congress, I hope to change things where your people are concerned. We can't rejoice about liberty and justice, it seems, until those values are granted to every citizen."

"Here, here," William chanted. "Is this the Jared Mifflin I met back in May?"

"It is, my friend. You gave me a great deal to ponder, and I hope I did the same for you."

William knew what Jared was referring to but chose to make his farewells and be off. "If any of you decide to visit Boston, or better yet, to settle in the great state of Massachusetts, I'd be delighted to put you up. Right now, I've got a job to do." His voice cracked, but he quickly regained his composure by pumping his friends' hands. To Hetty he offered a gallant bow, after which he took her dainty hand in his and softly kissed it.

"Whew!" the other two boys exclaimed. Without further comment, William took off for his waiting horse and soon was gone.

"Henry," Mr. Baldwin called out as he approached the group, "be sure and have everything packed up by the morning. We'll leave at the crack of dawn."

"Yessuh," Henry said, turning back to Hetty and Jared to say farewell.

EPILOGUE

"MASTER Mifflin! Master Mifflin!" the coachman called through the side window.

"What?" Jared heard himself mumble. His eyes opened slowly. The carriage had come to a standstill, and his trunks were being unloaded from the top of the roof.

Gazing out at the beautifully manicured grounds and magnificent stone buildings before him, Jared realized where he was.

"We're here, master," the coachman said. "Princeton, New Jersey, it is! Mighty sound sleeper you are. The last leg of the journey was pretty rough, but it didn't seem to bother you! You must have had quite a time last night, aye?" he said with a cackle. A steward appeared and hoisted one of Jared's trunks onto his shoulders.

"Yes, indeed, sir," Jared answered, going along with the coachman, "it certainly was quite a night . . . as a matter of fact, it was quite a summer!"

Jared descended the two steps from the carriage. Placing a few shillings into the driver's hand, he patted his waistcoat pocket to make sure that Hetty's letter was still there and proceeded to follow the steward across the courtyard.

He couldn't account for all his emotions, although he was experiencing many. His tattered copy of *Common Sense*, which was tucked into his back pocket, rubbed against him as a sort of reminder, he felt, of the work he had ahead of him. If he had learned only one thing from the Constitutional Convention, it was that the seventeenth of September was only a beginning for this new nation. Now it was up to his friends—the old ones and the new—to support the struggle while continuing to work for liberty and justice for all.

He took a deep breath. The country air smelled fresh and good. With Hetty waiting for him at home and the spirit of his father guiding his every move, Jared was eager to tackle whatever the future held.

Imprinted on his mind was a comment made by Dr. Franklin just as he and Hetty were leaving the State House Yard for the last time that summer. An elderly peasant woman shouted at the good doctor: "Well, Mr. Franklin," she asked, "what have we got, a republic or a monarchy?"

And Dr. Franklin replied, "A republic, if you can keep it!"

Jared skipped up the steps that led to his dormitory room two at a time. "I'll keep it, Dr. Franklin," he said out loud, "I'll keep it, indeed!"

BIBLIOGRAPHY

The American Philosophical Society. *Historic Philadelphia: From the Founding until the Early 19th Century*, Vol. 43, pt. 1. Philadelphia: The American Philosophical Society, 1953.

The American History Association and The American Political Science Association. *This Constitution for the U.S.A.: A Bicentennial Chronicle*, Project 87 for the Bicentennial of the U.S. Constitution. Vol. 4 (fall 1984). Washington D.C.: National Endowment for the Humanities, 1984.

——*This Constitution for the U.S.A.: A Bicentennial Chronicle*, Project 87 for the Bicentennial of the U.S. Constitution. Vol. 5 (winter 1985). Washington D.C.: National Endowment for the Humanities, 1985.

——*This Constitution for the U.S.A.: A Bicentennial Chronicle*, Project 87 for the Bicentennial of the U.S. Constitution. Vol. 7 (summer 1985). Washington D.C.: National Endowment for the Humanities, 1985.

Andrews, Charles McLean. *Colonial Folkways*. Northford, CT: Elliot's Books, 1919.

Commager, Henry Steele. *The Great Constitution*. New York: Bobbs-Merrill Co., 1961.

Cutler, William Parker and J. Perkins Cutler. *The Life, Journals and Correspondence of Rev. Manasseh Cutler, Lld*. Cincinnati, OH: Robert Clarke & Co., 1888.

Ferris, Robert, ed. *Signers of the Constitution*. Flagstaff, AZ: Interpretive Publications, 1986.

Ford, Paul Leicester. *The True George Washington*. Salem, NH: Ayer Company Publications, 1896.

Ford, Paul Leicester. *The Many Sided Franklin*. Salem, NH: Ayer Company Publications, 1898.

Kaminisky, John P. and Gaspare J. Saladino, ed. *The Documentary History of the Ratification of the Constitution: Commentaries on the Constitution: Public and Private*, Vol. 1. Madison: State Historical Society of Wisconsin, 1981.

Ketcham, Ralph. *James Madison: A Biography*. London: Macmillan Ltd., 1971.

Loeper, John J. *Going to School in 1776*. New York: Macmillan, 1984.

Madison, James. *Journal of the Federal Convention of 1787*. Edited by E. H. Scott. Salem, NH: Ayer Company Publications, 1908.

Paine, Thomas. *Common Sense*. New York: Penguin American Library, 1982.

Rossiter, Clinton. *1787: The Grand Convention*. New York: Macmillan, 1966.

Rossiter, Clinton. *The Final American Revolution: The American Colonies on the Eve of Independence*. New York: Harcourt Brace Jovanovich. 1956.

Stockham, Peter, ed. *The Little Book of Early American Crafts and Trades*. New York: Dover Publications, 1976.

Tuchman, Barbara. *The March of Folly: From Troy to Vietnam*. New York: Alfred A. Knopf, Inc., 1984.

Warden, Ann. "The Diary of Mrs. Ann Warden from June 1786–October 1788." *Pennsylvania Magazine of History and Biography*, Vol. 18, 1897.

Weigley, Russell F. et al., eds. *Philadelphia: A Three Hundred Year History*. New York: W. W. Norton & Co., 1982.

Zall, P. M., ed. *Ben Franklin Laughing: Anecdotes from Original Sources by and about Benjamin Franklin*. Berkeley: University of California Press, 1980.

APPENDIX

The Constitution
of the United States of America

PREAMBLE

We the People of the United States, in Order to form a more perfect Union, establish Justice, insure domestic Tranquility, provide for the common defense, promote the general Welfare, and secure the Blessings of Liberty to ourselves and our Posterity, do ordain and establish this Constitution for the United States of America.

ARTICLE I

SECTION 1. All legislative Powers herein granted shall be vested in a Congress of the United States, which shall consist of a Senate and House of Representatives.

SECTION 2. The House of Representatives shall be composed of Members chosen every second Year by the People of the several States, and the Electors in each State shall have the Qualifications requisite for Electors of the most numerous Branch of the State Legislature.

No Person shall be a Representative who shall not have attained to the Age of twenty-five Years, and been seven Years a Citizen of the United States, and who shall not, when elected, be an Inhabitant of that State in which he shall be chosen.

Representatives *and direct Taxes* shall be apportioned among the several States which may be included within this Union, according to their respective Numbers, *which shall be determined by adding to the whole Number of free Persons, including those bound to Service for a Term of Years, and excluding Indians not taxed, three fifths of all other Persons.* The actual Enumeration shall be made within three Years after the first Meeting of the Congress of the United States, and within every subsequent Term of ten Years, in such Manner as they shall by Law direct. The Number of Representatives shall not exceed one for every thirty Thousand, but each State shall have at Least one Representative; *and until such enumeration shall be made, the State of New Hampshire shall be entitled to choose three; Massachusetts eight; Rhode Island and Providence Plantations one; Connecticut five; New York six; New Jersey four; Pennsylvania eight; Delaware one; Maryland six; Virginia ten; North Carolina five; South Carolina five; and Georgia three.*

When vacancies happen in the Representation from any State, the Executive Authority thereof shall issue Writs of Election to fill such Vacancies.

The House of Representatives shall choose their Speaker and other Officers; and shall have the sole Power of Impeachment.

SECTION 3. The Senate of the United States shall be composed of two Senators from each State, *chosen by the Legislature thereof*, for six Years; and each Senator shall have one Vote.

Immediately after they shall be assembled in Consequence of the first Election, they shall be divided as equally as may be into three Classes. The Seats of the Senators of the first Class shall be vacated at the Expiration of the second Year, of the second Class at the Expiration of the fourth Year, and of the third Class at the Expiration of the sixth Year, so that one third may be chosen every second Year; and if Vacancies happen by Resignation, or otherwise, during the Recess of the Legislature of any State, the Executive thereof may make temporary Appointments until the next Meeting of the Legislature, which shall then fill such Vacancies.

No Person shall be a Senator who shall not have attained to the Age of thirty Years, and been nine Years a Citizen of the United States, and who shall not, when elected, be an Inhabitant of that State for which he shall be chosen.

The Vice President of the United States shall be President of the Senate, but shall have no Vote, unless they be equally divided.

The Senate shall choose their other Officers, and also a President pro tempore, in the Absence of the Vice President, or when he shall exercise the Office of President of the United States.

The Senate shall have the sole Power to try all Impeachments. When sitting for that Purpose, they shall be on Oath or Affirmation. When the President of the United States is tried, the Chief Justice shall preside: And no Person shall be convicted without the Concurrence of two thirds of the Members present.

Judgment in Cases of Impeachment shall not extend further than to removal from Office, and disqualification to hold and enjoy any Office of honor, Trust or Profit under the United States: but the Party convicted shall nevertheless be liable and subject to Indictment, Trial, Judgment and Punishment, according to Law.

SECTION 4. The Times, Places and Manner of holding Elections for Senators and Representatives, shall be prescribed in each State by the Legislature thereof; but the Congress may at any time by Law make or alter such Regulations, except as to the Places of choosing Senators.

The Congress shall assemble at least once in every Year, *and such Meeting shall be on the first Monday in December, unless they shall by Law appoint a different Day.*

SECTION 5. Each House shall be the Judge of the Elections, Returns and Qualifications of its own Members, and a Majority of each shall constitute a Quorum to do Business; but a smaller Number may adjourn from day to day, and may be authorized to compel the Attendance of absent Members, in such Manner, and under such Penalties as each House may provide.

Each House may determine the Rules of its Proceedings, punish its Members for disorderly Behavior, and, with the Concurrence of two thirds, expel a Member.

Each House shall keep a Journal of its Proceedings, and from time to time publish the same, excepting such Parts as may in their Judgment require Secrecy; and the Yeas and Nays of the Members of either House on any question shall, at the Desire of one fifth of those Present, be entered on the Journal.

Neither House, during the Session of Congress, shall, without the Consent of the other, adjourn for more than three days, nor to any other Place than that in which the two Houses shall be sitting.

SECTION 6. The Senators and Representatives shall receive a Compensation for their Services, to be ascertained by Law, and paid out of the Treasury of the United States. They shall in all Cases, except Treason, Felony and Breach of the Peace, be privileged from Arrest during their Attendance at the Session of their respective Houses, and in going to and returning from the same; and for any Speech or Debate in either House, they shall not be questioned in any other Place.

No Senator or Representative shall, during the Time for which he was elected, be appointed to any civil Office under the Authority of the United States, which shall have been created, or the Emoluments whereof shall have been increased during such time; and no Person holding any Office under the United States, shall be a Member of either House during his Continuance in Office.

SECTION 7. All Bills for raising Revenue shall originate in the House of Representatives; but the Senate may propose or concur with Amendments as on other Bills.

Every Bill which shall have passed the House of Representatives and the Senate, shall, before it become a Law, be presented to the President of the United States; If he approve he shall sign it, but if not he shall return it, with his Objections to that House in which it shall have originated, who shall enter the Objections at large on their Journal, and proceed to reconsider it. If after such Reconsideration two thirds of that House shall agree to pass the Bill, it shall be sent, together with the Objections, to the other House, by which it shall likewise be reconsidered, and if approved by two thirds of that House, it shall become a Law. But in all such Cases the Votes of both Houses shall be determined by Yeas and Nays, and the Names of the Persons voting for and against the Bill shall be entered on the Journal of each House respectively. If any Bill shall not be returned by the President within ten Days (Sundays excepted) after it shall have been presented to him, the Same shall be a Law, in like Manner as if he had signed it, unless the Congress by their Adjournment prevent its Return, in which Case it shall not be a Law.

Every Order, Resolution, or Vote to which the Concurrence of the Senate and House of Representatives may be necessary (except on a question of Adjournment) shall be presented to the President of the United States; and before the Same shall take Effect, shall be approved by him, or being disapproved by him, shall be repassed by two thirds of the Senate and House of Representatives, according to the Rules and Limitations prescribed in the Case of a Bill.

SECTION 8. The Congress shall have Power To lay and collect Taxes, Duties, Imposts and Excises, to pay the Debts and provide for the common Defense and general Welfare of the United States; but all Duties, Imposts and Excises shall be uniform throughout the United States;

To borrow Money on the credit of the United States;

To regulate Commerce with foreign Nations, and among the several States, and with the Indian Tribes;

To establish an uniform Rule of Naturalization, and uniform Laws on the subject of Bankruptcies throughout the United States;

To coin Money, regulate the Value thereof, and of foreign Coin, and fix the Standard of Weights and Measures;

To provide for the Punishment of counterfeiting the Securities and current Coin of the United States;

To establish Post Offices and post Roads;

To promote the Progress of Science and useful Arts, by securing for limited Times to Authors and Inventors the exclusive Right to their respective Writings and Discoveries;

To constitute Tribunals inferior to the supreme Court;

To define and punish Piracies and Felonies committed on the high Seas, and Offences against the Law of Nations;

To declare War, grant Letters of Marque and Reprisal, and make Rules concerning Captures on Land and Water;

To raise and support Armies, but no Appropriation of Money to that Use shall be for a longer Term than two Years;

To provide and maintain a Navy;

To make Rules for the Government and Regulation of the land and naval Forces;

To provide for calling forth the Militia to execute the Laws of the Union, suppress Insurrections and repel Invasions;

To provide for organizing, arming, and disciplining, the Militia, and for governing such Part of them as may be employed in the Service of the United States, reserving to the States respectively, the Appointment of the Officers, and the Authority of training the Militia according to the discipline prescribed by Congress.

To exercise exclusive Legislation in all Cases whatsoever, over such District (not exceeding ten Miles square) as may, by Cession of particular States, and the Acceptance of Congress, become the Seat of the Government of the United States, and to exercise like Authority over all Places purchased by the Consent of the Legislature of the State in which the Same shall be, for the Erection of Forts, Magazines, Arsenals, dock-Yards, and other needful Buildings;—And

To make all Laws which shall be necessary and proper for carrying into Execution the foregoing Powers, and all other Powers vested by this Constitution in the Government of the United States, or in any Department or Officer thereof.

SECTION 9. *The Migration or Importation of such Persons as any of the States now existing shall think proper to admit, shall not be prohibited by the Congress prior to the Year one thousand eight hundred and eight, but a Tax or duty may be imposed on such Importation, not exceeding ten dollars for each Person.*

The Privilege of the Writ of Habeas Corpus shall not be suspended, unless when in Cases of Rebellion or Invasion the public Safety may require it.

No Bill of Attainder or ex post facto Law shall be passed.

No Capitation, or other direct, Tax shall be laid, unless in Proportion to the Census or Enumeration herein before directed to be taken.

No Tax or Duty shall be laid on Articles exported from any state.

No Preference shall be given by any Regulation of Commerce or Revenue to the Ports of one State over those of another: nor shall Vessels bound to, or from, one State, be obliged to enter, clear, or pay Duties in another.

No Money shall be drawn from the Treasury, but in Consequence of Appropriations made by Law; and a regular Statement and Account of the Receipts and Expenditures of all public Money shall be published from time to time.

No Title of Nobility shall be granted by the United States: And no Person holding any Office of Profit or Trust under them, shall, without the Consent of the Congress, accept of any present, Emolument, Office, or Title, of any kind whatever, from any King, Prince, or foreign State.

SECTION 10. No State shall enter into any Treaty, Alliance, or Confederation; grant Letters of Marque and Reprisal; coin Money; emit Bills of Credit; make any Thing but gold and silver Coin a Tender in Payment of Debts; pass any Bill of Attainder, ex post facto Law, or Law impairing the Obligation of Contracts, or grant any Title of Nobility.

No State shall, without the Consent of the Congress, lay any Imposts or Duties on Imports or Exports, except what may be absolutely necessary for executing its inspection Laws: and the net Produce of all Duties and Imposts, laid by any Senate on Imports or Exports, shall be for the Use of the Treasury of the United States; and all such Laws shall be subject to the Revision and Control of the Congress.

No State shall, without the Consent of Congress, lay any Duty of Tonnage, keep Troops, or Ships of War in time of Peace, enter into any Agreement or Compact with another State, or with a foreign Power, or engage in War, unless actually invaded, or in such imminent Danger as will not admit of delay.

ARTICLE II

SECTION 1. The executive Power shall be vested in a President of the United States of America. He shall hold his Office during the Term of four Years, and, together with the Vice President, chosen for the same Term, be elected, as follows.

Each State shall appoint, in such Manner as the Legislature thereof may direct, a Number of Electors, equal to the whole Number of Senators and Representatives to which the State may be entitled in the Congress: but no Senator or Representative, or Person holding an Office of Trust or Profit under the United States, shall be appointed an Elector.

The Electors shall meet in their respective States, and vote by Ballot for two Persons, of whom one at least shall not be an Inhabitant of the same State with themselves. And they shall make a List of all the Persons voted for, and of the Number of Votes for each; which List they shall sign and certify, and transmit sealed to the Seat of the Government of the United States, directed to the President of the Senate. The President of the Senate shall, in the Presence of the Senate and House of Representatives, open all the Certificates, and the Votes shall then be counted. The Person having the greatest Number of Votes shall be the President, if such Number be a

Majority of the whole Number of Electors appointed; and if there be more than one who have such majority, and have an equal Number of Votes, then the House of Representatives shall immediately choose by Ballot one of them for President; and if no Person have a Majority, then from the five highest on the List the said House shall in like Manner choose the President. But in choosing the President, the Votes shall be taken by States, the Representation from each State having one Vote; A quorum for this Purpose shall consist of a Member or Members from two thirds of the States, and a Majority of all the States shall be necessary to a Choice. In every Case, after the Choice of the President, the Person having the greatest Number of Votes of the Electors shall be the Vice President. But if there should remain two or more who have equal Votes, the Senate shall choose from them by Ballot the Vice President.

The Congress may determine the Time of choosing the Electors, and the Day on which they shall give their Votes; which Day shall be the same throughout the United States.

No Person except a natural born Citizen, or a Citizen of the United States, at the time of the Adoption of this Constitution, shall be eligible to the Office of President; neither shall any Person be eligible to that Office who shall not have attained to the Age of thirty-five Years, and been fourteen Years a Resident within the United States.

In Case of the Removal of the President from Office, or of his Death, Resignation, or Inability to discharge the Powers and Duties of the said Office, the Same shall devolve on the Vice President, and the Congress may by Law provide for the Case of Removal, Death, Resignation or Inability, both of the President and Vice President, declaring what Officer shall then act as President, and such Officer shall act accordingly, until the Disability be removed, or a President shall be elected.

The President shall, at stated Times, receive for his Services, a Compensation, which shall neither be increased nor diminished during the Period for which he shall have been elected, and he shall not receive within that Period any other Emolument from the United States, or any of them.

Before he enter on the Execution of his Office, he shall take the following Oath or Affirmation:—"I do solemnly swear (or affirm) that I will faithfully execute the Office of President of the United States, and will to the best of my Ability, preserve, protect and defend the Constitution of the United States."

SECTION 2. The President shall be Commander in Chief of the Army and Navy of the United States, and of the Militia of the several States, when called into the actual Service of the United States; he may require the Opinion, in writing, of the principal Officer in each of the executive Departments, upon any Subject relating to the Duties of their respective Offices, and he shall have Power to grant Reprieves and Pardons for Offenses against the United States, except in Cases of Impeachment.

He shall have Power, by and with the Advice and Consent of the Senate, to make Treaties, provided two thirds of the Senators present concur; and he shall nominate, and by and with the Advice and Consent of the Senate, shall appoint Ambassadors, other public Ministers and Consuls, Judges of the supreme Court, and all other Officers of the United States, whose Appointments are not herein otherwise provided for, and which shall be established by Law: but the Congress may by Law vest the Appointment of such inferior Officers, as they think proper, in the President alone, in the Courts of Law, or in the Heads of Departments.

The President shall have Power to fill up all Vacancies that may happen during the Recess of the Senate, by granting Commissions which shall expire at the End of their next Session.

SECTION 3. He shall from time to time give to the Congress Information of the State of the Union, and recommend to their Consideration such Measures as he shall judge necessary and expedient; he may, on extraordinary Occasions, convene both Houses, or either of them, and in Case of Disagreement between them, with Respect to the Time of Adjournment, he may adjourn them to such Time as he shall think proper; he shall receive Ambassadors and other public Ministers; he shall take Care that the Laws be faithfully executed, and shall Commission all the Officers of the United States.

SECTION 4. The President, Vice President and all civil Officers of the United States, shall be removed from Office on Impeachment for, and Conviction of, Treason, Bribery, or other high Crimes and Misdemeanors.

ARTICLE III

SECTION 1. The judicial Power of the United States, shall be vested in one supreme Court, and in such inferior Courts as the Congress may from time to time ordain and establish. The Judges, both of the supreme and inferior Courts, shall hold their Offices during good Behavior, and shall, at stated Times, receive for their Services, a Compensation, which shall not be diminished during their Continuance in Office.

SECTION 2. The judicial Power shall extend to all Cases, in Law and Equity, arising under this Constitution, the Laws of the United States, and Treaties made, or which shall be made, under their Authority;—to all Cases affecting Ambassadors, other public Ministers and Consuls;—to all Cases of admiralty and maritime Jurisdiction;—to Controversies to which the United States shall be a Party;—to Controversies between two or more States;—*between a State and Citizens of another state;*— between Citizens of different States;—between Citizens of the same State claiming Lands under Grants of different States, *and between a State, or the Citizens thereof, and foreign States, Citizens or Subjects.*

In all Cases affecting Ambassadors, other public Ministers and Consuls, and those in which a State shall be Party, the supreme Court shall have original Jurisdiction. In all the other Cases before mentioned, the supreme Court shall have appellate Jurisdiction, both as to Law and Fact, with such Exceptions, and under such Regulations as the Congress shall make.

The Trial of all Crimes, except in Cases of Impeachment, shall be by Jury; and such Trial shall be held in the State where the said Crimes shall have been committed; but when not committed within any State, the Trial shall be at such Place or Places as the Congress may by Law have directed.

SECTION 3. Treason against the United States, shall consist only in levying War against them, or in adhering to their Enemies, giving them Aid and Comfort. No Person shall be convicted of Treason unless on the Testimony of two Witnesses to the same overt Act, or on Confession in open Court.

The Congress shall have Power to declare the Punishment of Treason, but no Attainder of Treason shall work Corruption of Blood, or Forfeiture except during the Life of the Person attainted.

ARTICLE IV

SECTION 1. Full Faith and Credit shall be given in each State to the public Acts, Records, and judicial Proceedings of every other State. And the Congress may by general Laws prescribe the Manner in which such Acts, Records and Proceedings shall be proved, and the Effect thereof.

SECTION 2. The Citizens of each State shall be entitled to all Privileges and Immunities of Citizens in the several States.

A Person charged in any State with Treason, Felony, or other Crime, who shall flee from Justice, and be found in another State, shall on Demand of the executive Authority of the State from which he fled, be delivered up, to be removed to the State having Jurisdiction of the Crime.

No Person held to Service of Labor in one State, under the Laws thereof, escaping into another, shall, in Consequence of any Law or Regulation therein, be discharged from such Service or Labor, but shall be delivered up on Claim of the Party to whom such Service or Labor may be due.

SECTION 3. New States may be admitted by the Congress into this Union; but no new State shall be formed or erected within the Jurisdiction of any other State; nor any State be formed by the Junction of two or more States, or Parts of States, without the Consent of the Legislatures of the States concerned as well as of the Congress.

The Congress shall have Power to dispose of and make all needful Rules and Regulations respecting the Territory or other Property belonging to the United States; and nothing in this Constitution shall be so construed as to Prejudice any Claims of the United States, or of any particular State.

SECTION 4. The United States shall guarantee to every State in this Union a Republican Form of Government, and shall protect each of them against Invasion; and on Application of the Legislature, or of the Executive (when the Legislature cannot be convened) against domestic Violence.

ARTICLE V

The Congress, whenever two thirds of both Houses shall deem it necessary, shall propose Amendments to this Constitution, or, on the Application of the Legislatures of two thirds of the several States, shall call a Convention for proposing Amendments, which, in either Case, shall be valid to all Intents and Purposes, as Part of this Constitution, when ratified by the Legislatures of three fourths of the several States, or by Conventions in three fourths thereof, as the one or the other Mode of Ratification may be proposed by the Congress; Provided that no Amendment which may be made prior to the Year One thousand eight hundred and eight shall in any Manner affect the first and fourth Clauses in the Ninth Section of the first Article; and that no State, without its Consent, shall be deprived of its equal Suffrage in the Senate.

ARTICLE VI

All Debts contracted and Engagements entered into, before the Adoption of this Constitution, shall be as valid against the United States under this Constitution, as under the Confederation.

This Constitution, and the Laws of the United States which shall be made in Pursuance thereof; and all Treaties made, or which shall be made, under the Authority of the United States, shall be the supreme Law of the Land; and the Judges in every State shall be bound thereby, any Thing in the Constitution or Laws of any State to the Contrary notwithstanding.

The Senators and Representatives before mentioned, and the Members of the several State Legislatures, and all executive and judicial Officers, both of the United States and of the several States, shall be bound by Oath or Affirmation, to support this Constitution; but no religious Test shall ever be required as a Qualification to any Office or public Trust under the United States.

ARTICLE VII

The Ratification of the Conventions of nine States, shall be sufficient for the Establishment of this Constitution between the States so ratifying the Same.

DONE in Convention by the Unanimous Consent of the States present the Seventeenth Day of September in the Year of our Lord one thousand seven hundred and Eighty seven and of the Independence of the United States of America the Twelfth. IN WITNESS whereof We have hereunto subscribed our Names.

George Washington—
PRESIDENT AND DEPUTY FROM VIRGINIA

NEW HAMPSHIRE
John Langdon
Nicholas Gilman

MASSACHUSETTS
Nathaniel Gorham
Rufus King

CONNECTICUT
William Samuel Johnson
Roger Sherman

NEW YORK
Alexander Hamilton

NEW JERSEY
William Livingston
David Brearley
William Paterson
Jonathan Dayton

PENNSYLVANIA
Benjamin Franklin
Thomas Mifflin
Robert Morris
George Clymer
Thomas FitzSimons
Jared Ingersoll
James Wilson
Gouverneur Morris

DELAWARE
George Read
Gunning Bedford, Jr.
John Dickinson
Richard Bassett
Jacob Broom

MARYLAND
James McHenry
Daniel of St. Thomas Jenifer
Daniel Carroll

VIRGINIA
John Blair
James Madison, Jr.

NORTH CAROLINA
William Blount
Richard Dobbs Spaight
Hugh Williamson

SOUTH CAROLINA
John Rutledge
Charles Cotesworth Pinckney
Charles Pinckney
Pierce Butler

GEORGIA
William Few
Abraham Baldwin

ATTEST: William Jackson, SECRETARY

(Italicized material has been deleted from the Constitution by time limits or by amendments.)